Foreword by George Grant

# Six Voices, One Story

## The Heart of AmblesideOnline

Written by the AmblesideOnline Advisory

Paperback Version:
ISBN 9798399947532
Hardcover Version:
ISBN: 9798860796676
Imprint: Independently published

Photo credit: Harris Beauchamp

The cover features “Snakeshead,” a textile design created by William Morris in the 1870s. Snakeshead is a flowering plant, *Fritillaria meleagris*, which used to grow abundantly but is now found in only a few spots in England. Morris's views on art, homes, and nature influenced Charlotte Mason, and his work is a favorite of the Advisory. (Cover design by KingdomCovers.com)

# Dedication

We dedicate this book to the families worldwide who use our AmblesideOnline curriculum and to their children.
For the children's sake, for Jesus' sake.

# Table of Contents

# Acknowledgments

The endeavor that is AmblesideOnline has been entrusted to us, but we have not labored alone. From its inception, there have been willing helpers who have come alongside us with their time, their expertise, their wisdom, and their prayers. Some have labored for a season, while others are with us still.

Because we could not name them all without the risk of missing a few of those who have contributed, we must allow their names to go unmentioned. But for every mom who typed or proofread an article for the website, every family who tested out a book or idea, every friend who answered a question or shared an experience—we are thankful for each and every one of you. Contemplating the number of wise and dedicated helpers we have been privileged to know is humbling. There are so many!

AmblesideOnline would not be all that it is without the continuing faithful help of each of these, who share our love of Charlotte Mason's ideas and our vision for an education for all. We are so grateful for the large company of friends who have joined us in this venture, and we trust that the Lord will bless you as you have blessed us.

# Foreword

## A Wider Diameter of Light

During the Christmas holidays in 1841, Thomas Chalmers paid a visit to the tiny Borders town of Skirling in Peeblesshire. The author, educator, reformer, theologian, and orator was then perhaps the most prominent man in all of Scotland. So his visit was quite an extraordinary event. And even more extraordinarily, during his stay, he consented to stop by the local village school and give a lecture to its eleven students on mathematics.

The great man was always inclined to leave a moral philosophy lesson whenever he taught, even when he was teaching natural philosophy. And so it was that at the conclusion of his animated lecture, he drew a large circle on the slate board and declared:

> The wider a man's knowledge becomes, the deeper should be his humility; for the more he knows the more he sees of what remains unknown. The wider the diameter of light, the larger the circumference of darkness. And so, with every footstep of growing knowledge there ought to be a growing humility—that is the best guarantee both for a sound philosophy and a sound faith. (Moffatt, p. 352)

The importance of this vital lesson was not soon lost on his now awestruck hearers. The phrase "A Wider Diameter of Light" would become emblematic for them of the true purpose of education and the ultimate aim of the vibrant Christian life—a life deeply rooted in humility.

I'd like to think that Charlotte Mason would have immediately responded to Chalmers with a hearty "amen." It is after all likewise emblematic of her vision for a wide and generous education and life.

In a myriad of ways she affirmed the truth that genuine education is a form of repentance. It is a humble admission that we've not read all that we need to read, we don't know all that we need to know, and we've not yet become all that we are called to become. Education is that unique form of discipleship that brings us to the place of admitting our inadequacies. It is that remarkable rebuke of autonomy and independence so powerful and so evident that we actually slow down and pay heed for a change.

In A.A. Milne's *The House at Pooh Corner,* there is a delightful scene:

> "Well, I've got an idea," said Rabbit, "and here it is. We take Tigger for a long explore, somewhere where he's never been, and we lose him there, and next morning we find him again, and—mark my words—he'll be a different Tigger altogether."
>
> "Why?" said Pooh.
>
> "Because he'll be a Humble Tigger. Because he'll be a Sad Tigger, a Melancholy Tigger, a Small and Sorry Tigger, and an Oh-Rabbit-I-*am*-glad-to-see-you Tigger. That's why." (pp. 112–113)

Like Tigger, we all really need a long explore—frequently and persistently. That sort of long explore is precisely the vision for lifelong learning that Charlotte Mason affords us. And it is what AmblesideOnline has made practical and accessible over the course of more than two decades now so that we all can join Tigger in discovering a wider diameter of light.

This remarkable and beautiful book tells the story of six ordinary homeschooling moms and their ever-growing AmblesideOnline community as they ventured forth on a long explore together. It tells of their exultant joys and their disconsolate sorrows. It tells of their astonishment at the exceedingly rich inheritance of beauty, goodness, and truth they'd been given. It tells of their consequent profound gratitude and humility. It tells of the extraordinary web of relationships the Lord wove around them as they began to understand that true education is perhaps more about a culture than it is about a curriculum; that it is more about a way of life than it is merely a way of doing; that it is a vision of what God has called us to rather than a mechanical set of prescriptives; that it is about faith, family, and community; that it is about the rich covenant into which we have been engrafted by God's good providence.

Concluding his visit to the little one-room stone schoolhouse in Skirling, Thomas Chalmers bowed his head to pray for the young students—and for himself—saying:

> Let us no longer be deceived by the imagination of any strength or sufficiency in ourselves; but let us humbly look up to the very God of grace and peace, that He might sanctify us wholly and that henceforth, we may put off the unfruitful works of darkness and pride and put on instead His bright armor, amidst a wider diameter of light. (Moffatt, p. 352)

Herein is the heart and soul of education. Herein is the beginning of humble repentance.

Read this book and I am convinced you will experience all that I have as I read it: you will laugh; you will cry; you will be inspired; you will have aha moments; you will go running for your commonplace journal to capture incisive quotes; you will be encouraged; you will be prompted to embark on a long explore; you will gasp with wonder and awe at a wider diameter of light. *Tolle lege.*

*George Grant*
*Pastor, Parish Presbyterian Church*
*Franklin, Tennessee*

# Introduction

Welcome to our book.

We have been planning this for a long time. In fact, the first time that "writing our story" appeared as an official agenda item for an AmblesideOnline Educational Foundation board meeting was back in July of 2018. But even before that, we frequently mentioned how we wanted to write about AmblesideOnline from each of our perspectives, to the glory of God. And with *Six Voices, One Story: The Heart of AmblesideOnline*, that is still our objective.

We are the AmblesideOnline Advisory. That means we are the founders, creators, stewards, visionaries, and board members of AmblesideOnline.org, which we describe on our website as a "free Charlotte Mason curriculum" that "prepares children for a life of rich relationships with God, humanity, and the natural world." We are a band of mothers who followed God and these vitalizing ideas, and along the way were blessed with an enduring and extraordinary friendship.

There were six of us when we started writing the book. In fact, there were six of us up until February 2022: Donna-Jean Breckenridge, Lynn Bruce, Wendi Capehart, Karen Glass, Leslie Laurio, and Anne White. There are four of us now. That story of going from six to four is included here—but perhaps it's more important than ever to say that this book is still from all six of us.

Our work of curriculum planning has taken place almost entirely through letters. The letters have been (and continue to be) in the form of emailed correspondence, as our treasured times in person are rare. This book is a compilation of emails, blog posts, articles, and new material from the six of us, written over two decades in which we planned and created AmblesideOnline and also nurtured an enduring friendship.*

*Six Voices, One Story: The Heart of AmblesideOnline* tells about that planning and that relationship. Here is our history, our story, and our heart for "an education for all." We offer it humbly, with prayers for you and yours as you read.

The AmblesideOnline Advisory:
Donna-Jean Breckenridge
Karen Glass
Leslie Laurio
Anne White
and, ever in our hearts,
Lynn Bruce
and
Wendi Capehart

> Once we see that we are dealing spirit with spirit with the friend at whose side we are sitting, with the people who attend to our needs, we shall be able to realise how incessant is the commerce between the divine Spirit and our human spirit. It will be to us as when one stops one's talk and one's thoughts in the springtime, to find the world full of bird-music unheard the instant before. (*Parents and Children*, pp. 276–277)

---

* The material has been lightly edited for inclusion in this volume.

# I Have an Idea

(*Leslie Laurio, 1999*)

The brave things in the old tales and songs, Mr. Frodo: adventures, as I used to call them. I used to think that they were things the wonderful folk of the stories went out and looked for, because they wanted them, because they were exciting and life was a bit dull, a kind of a sport, as you might say. But that's not the way of it with the tales that really mattered, or the ones that stay in the mind. Folk seem to have been just landed in them, usually—their paths were laid that way, as you put it. (*The Two Towers* by J.R.R. Tolkien)

We cannot tell the precise moment when friendship is formed. As in filling a vessel drop by drop, there is at last a drop which makes it run over; so in a series of kindnesses there is at last one which makes the heart run over. (*The Life of Samuel Johnson, LL.D.* by James Boswell, Esq.)

## Donna-Jean: Our First Chapter

I was adamant.

"We are not bringing a computer into this house."

Looking back, I have no idea what I was thinking. We were not a homeschool family that did not have television, for example, like some of our friends. But this was back in the early 1990s, when I didn't know anyone who had a computer in their home, and I could not imagine how it would be of any benefit. I worried this new device would somehow take away from family time or make us less interested in the many books that lined the walls of our living room, bedrooms, hallways, and even the kitchen.

Turns out, I was wrong. And my husband teased me about it for years afterward.

Eventually, the computer came in. The big clunky machine sat atop a long folding table in the family room, with modems and cords spread everywhere. We were on dial-up, there were limitations, and the whole thing was rather confusing to me. World Wide Web? Web of what? (In full disclosure, I was just as skeptical about Twitter, now called "X," many years later. "Only 143 characters? To say what, exactly?" Clearly, I have no prophetic skills where technology is concerned.)

But my husband knew the path toward my heart fully embracing this behemoth that was thwarting my interior design scheme. He found the website for the Louvre Museum in Paris.

Night after night, for long hours after our children were asleep, I perused the world's most famous paintings and sculptures as if I were walking through that iconic building myself (something I had not done in real life, despite a summer missions trip to France in Bible college). For an entire week, I stayed up until three or four o'clock every morning, looking at image after image of art collections, reading about them in English and then in French. By the end of that week, the complete lack of sleep wore me down. I had to get back to fixing meals and teaching my kids. But I was convinced: the personal computer would stay.

It was not long after that when I discovered that other homeschoolers were online too. I even found message boards populated with other women who had not only heard of the British educator Charlotte Mason but were writing about her as well.

I had already read about Charlotte Mason several years before. I first heard about Mason back in February of 1986, when my oldest daughter was a one-month-old baby. My brother had given me a book as a gift. It was Susan Schaeffer Macaulay's *For the Children's Sake*. I knew of Macaulay's mother, Edith Schaeffer, whose wonderful book *Hidden Art* had influenced me greatly as a young woman in high school. And everyone in the Christian world at that time knew her father, Francis Schaeffer. I had heard him speak at a National Religious Broadcasters convention in Washington, D.C., and had watched his *How Should We Then Live* film series at our church. With my new book in hand, the baby and I settled in the rocking chair, and I began to read about a woman who would change the course of my life.

The author told of her and her husband's quest to find a suitable school for their little girl while they were living in London. Nothing was quite right until they found a wonderful small school that was based upon Charlotte Mason's ideas. She then began to read the writings of Mason. (They were out of print by the time Macaulay wrote the book, which was disappointing news to me.) But Macaulay said that these ideas were "of such universal nature that one can apply them equally well at home, in different kinds of schools, in an orphanage in Africa, in an Indian village, in an inner-city school or day-care center" (p. 5).

Macaulay told of Charlotte Mason's foundational belief that "biblical Christianity is truth" and of her passionate credo that "children are born persons." As I read this the first time, I rocked and continued nodding in agreement, even as the little one in my arms shifted in sleep.

I read that Mason suffered greatly in her life; both parents died suddenly when she was just sixteen. And I read how she got into England's one teacher training college for women, only to have to leave a year later to take a job teaching at a small school while continuing her own lessons in her off-hours.

Along the way, Charlotte Mason prepared and gave lectures to parents about education. Despite her ill health, she persevered in her studies, and soon she founded the Parents' National Educational Union schools. Mason also founded the House of Education, her teacher training college, in Ambleside in England's Lake District.

My rocking slowed as my mind made a special connection to Charlotte Mason. My father's mother was born and raised in the Lake District. I grew up hearing the lilt of her accent, her love for her "countrymen" (as she referred to the poets she read and quoted so often), and the engaging stories of her childhood. My Mimi never forgot the island nation she left at the age of eighteen, and she taught her children and grandchildren to love it too. I wondered if she had been to a Charlotte Mason school or if she had been influenced by Mason in any way. I never found out for sure, but I liked thinking about it.

By the time I finished reading *For the Children's Sake* (the title comes from the motto of Charlotte Mason's college), I had learned a distilled version of Charlotte Mason's educational philosophy:

- "Children are born persons." What a thing to think of, looking down in wonder at my little daughter. She was her own person, and I had been given the magnificent privilege of watching her life unfold.

- Children should be given great books, not "twaddle," and be encouraged to narrate back what they have read. I thought of the small library I had built in my bedroom as a child—made up of Scholastic Book Club titles, Christmas and birthday gifts, and books that came from my mother's and grandmother's childhoods—and I knew that an education of great books was what I wanted for my daughter.

- Children, just like parents, are sinners under authority. Macaulay quoted Mason: "We need not add that authority is just and faithful in all matters of promise-keeping; it is also considerate, and that is why a good mother is the best home-ruler; she is in touch with the children. . . . Let us not despise the day of small things nor grow weary in well-doing . . ." (*School Education,* p. 23). I reflected upon my Mom and Dad and their dependence upon God, and I prayed I would somehow parent with that same level of reliance upon the Lord.

- "Education is an atmosphere, a discipline, and a life." This sentence would become C.M. 101 to later homeschool moms studying Charlotte Mason, but this was my first reading of it, my first understanding of its power. I read about the educational value of the child's natural home atmosphere, the discipline of habits of mind and body, the exciting concept that the brain adapts to "habitual lines of thought," and the need of "intellectual and moral as well as of physical sustenance." Then these words jumped out at me: "The mind feeds on ideas, and therefore children should have a generous curriculum." My job was not just to feed this little one in my arms a nutrition-rich diet; I was charged with feeding her mind as well.

- "Education is the science of relations." Those three nouns seemed disconnected, yet Mason pulled them together. She added a quote from her countryman Wordsworth's work, *The Prelude*: "Those first-born affinities that fit our new existence to existing things," to explain a child's natural relations with a vast number of things and thoughts: nature, handicrafts, science, art, and many living books. Or as our AmblesideOnline website would put it years later, "a life of rich relationships with God, humanity, and the natural world."

- "The Way of the Will and the Way of Reason." This described the impact of diversion (I thought of Romans chapter twelve and the directive there for a Christian to renew his mind) and the importance of not leaning on our own understanding. (Charlotte Mason's Bible knowledge showed in her writing, as she often incorporated Biblical phrases, such as this familiar verse from Proverbs chapter three.)
- Charlotte Mason's motto: "I am, I can, I ought, I will." It was tempting to fill in the sentences, to add the direct objects that seemed to be missing. But somehow these four phrases by themselves, without further explanation, held up the entire philosophy like pillars. (Charlotte Mason quotations are taken from her principles, as I first encountered them in *For the Children's Sake.*)

Charlotte Mason wanted students to come into direct contact with great minds, with the world around them, and with God Himself. I had never heard of Mason's ideas before that point, but they made sense to me. The best part of my own education was what took place outside of the classroom—the wonderful books of literature and history that I read at home, the exposure to God's creation all around me, the times a friend and I sat and studied our favorite Impressionist paintings, the stack of classical music record albums I listened to on so many afternoons, the poetry I memorized as a young girl, the hymns I sang in church, and the truths of the Bible that I learned from sitting under my pastor-father's weekly messages. The challenge for me would be how to take these aspects, along with my understanding of Charlotte Mason's educational principles, and have them form the framework of my child's schooling.

Once I finished the book, I did not linger too long on pondering the specifics of my little baby's educational future. She was a month old. School felt like science fiction, light years away.

But I never forgot all I had read in *For the Children's Sake*. A few years later, thanks to Dean and Karen Andreola, who also read Macaulay's book and sought to have Mason's works republished, the six volumes were back in print. And when a flyer came in the mail from the Conservative Book Club announcing a special membership drive with the lure "Get the six-volume *Original Homeschooling Series* by Charlotte Mason for free!", I signed on. A dangerous thing, those book clubs, but it was worth it.

As my daughter approached school age, the decision to homeschool sort of fell upon us. Initially it was not due to a great conviction about homeschooling itself. We wanted to send her to a Christian school, but we could not afford it. That was the extent of it.

My early teaching efforts included running our little homeschool with our only child as a sort of school-at-home, complete with bulletin board, textbooks, and lots of hands-on projects. We went to any and every outside activity that the local Christian homeschool support group held. We went on field trips to the fire department, an air traffic control tower, historical reenactments, nature centers, the mineral mines, the Seeing Eye, anywhere George Washington had been (this is New Jersey, after all), orchestra and theater performances, and several children's museums. We participated in weekly swim class, bowling, gymnastics, and ice skating. We learned whatever skill any mom in the group wanted to teach. And we had fun doing it.

But all along, as Bethany was in preschool, kindergarten, and first grade, I was doing a slow read of the pink-covered Charlotte Mason Series. And as I read and took notes, I gained the confidence to incorporate more of Mason's ideas. I eliminated textbooks, employed more "living books," required more and more narration (oral at first, and then added written narration as my daughter got older), included weekly exposure to great works of art and music as well as nature study, and gradually shaped my own curriculum plan for my daughter. By now we had a little son too, and soon there followed another baby girl. Several years later, another son would join our family. We had formed our family through birth and through adoption (both in the United States and from the Democratic Republic of Congo). And Charlotte Mason's ideas continued to fit our every situation.

I knew no one else personally who studied Mason's works. Other than the Series, only a couple of books on Charlotte Mason were available. And when it was time for our support group to showcase the different approaches to homeschooling (whether this or that textbook company, or the various popular unit study packages), I was the only one to talk about Charlotte Mason. I invited women to little meetings in my home to present her ideas, and we had a few sessions of studying the Series together.

After the online message boards came email lists, focused fully on Mason and her writing. It was thrilling to read post after post by women who were equally convinced that this was the best way to homeschool and to read how they were trying to make it happen. We shared book ideas, many narration samples, what we called "C.M. Moments" of when it all went well, and encouragement for when there were hard days. We talked about what to do for nature study when it was freezing cold outside or for those who lived in less nature-filled areas. We told funny stories of days gone terribly wrong. And we prayed for one another—even if we didn't know the person's full name or all the circumstances.

In those days, many were leery of posting their last names, and most were careful not to use their children's names at all. We referred to children as "ds" and "dd" (dear son and dear daughter), and as "10 yos, 8 yod, 6 yod" (10-year-old son, 8-year-old daughter, 6-year-old daughter). There were no photos—nothing at all that gave a hint of what the person looked like. Posts would end with a single first name, or sometimes just initials, or maybe a name and a little description. I began to recognize women whose posts were always, always worth reading—women like Anne (I first thought from her email address that she was in California until I realized that the "ca" meant Canada and she was Canadian), Karen in Krakow (How cool was that?), Wendi ("Mom of 7"), and Leslie Noelani with the Hawaiian name—and I read anything and everything from a woman named Lynn. These women wrote about their studies in Charlotte Mason's books and how they were implementing what they had discovered. They were brilliant, and I soaked up their every word. There were others too—women like Sheila, Ann in Faith, Leslie S., Cindy, Kim, Jeannette, Jackie, Amy, two women named Donna, and so many more. I got to know their writing styles, and I looked forward to their posts. I often printed out much of the information I read there, as well as the many beautifully written essays on different C.M.-related topics, and I collected them in a binder.

Lynn Hocraffer was the list-mama for all those years, and she ran it expertly. She set a schedule for going through the Series chapter by chapter, and she also moderated general topics like narration, picture study, C.M.-directed math, or poetry. She always left room for prayer requests, and she set aside one week a year for selling C.M.-compatible books. I still recall her "Tap, tap, tap…" in the subject line when she had to redirect us to the list's rules.

It felt like a movement, and it began to grow. One day, a few of the main writers announced they were starting a spin-off list, solely to study the C.M. Series more in-depth. I joined it and read along. And not long after, a new endeavor was presented.

The premise was to duplicate a C.M. education, as specifically as possible, given modern parameters. It was an exciting proposition, and I applauded the effort. I felt, though, that it was not something I could do. The little baby I had rocked in my arms while I read *For the Children's Sake* would soon begin high school, which was far past the grades being discussed. My son was also being homeschooled with books I had chosen specifically as we worked through his dyslexia, and my younger daughter was just preschool age. But what I really needed was a high school plan.

Many of the people on the list who had begun to use Charlotte Mason's ideas for their homeschool switched to something different for the high school years. Perhaps it was because there was nothing written online to follow. Perhaps it was because some were concerned about preparing for standardized testing and for college entry and wondered if a C.M. education was academically stringent enough. Or maybe it was because some still viewed Charlotte Mason's ideas as too gentle and easy-going, more suitable for younger children than high schoolers.

But none of that made sense to me. I had read the Series; I knew this education was more than nature walks and looking at paintings, as important as those things were. Charlotte Mason's principles were universal, her books had examples of impressive work done by upper-level students, and it seemed that switching to another method at this point was to throw away the harvest from the younger years. So I set out to write my own C.M.-based four-year high school curriculum and posted it on a website I had at the time.

The group that was putting together the C.M. curriculum called their leadership team the Advisory. In early 2001, I was asked to join, partly because of my focus on the high school years. The name of the project became AmblesideOnline (AO), and after much intense work, we were ready to publish. Opening day had a significant date: July 4, 2001.

The website was plain, without a lot of bells and whistles. We were keenly aware of families worldwide, missionaries in particular, who lived in places where internet connections were spotty or who got online only after traveling a distance to an internet café. We did not want the site to take too long loading or to cause any kind of problem for the viewer. We wanted nothing to stand in the way of it reaching anyone, anywhere, who wanted it. We did the work without any financial remuneration, and we also wanted the curriculum to be free forever. Charlotte Mason's vision of a "liberal education for all" meant, to us, that we would always make it available to anyone who could use it.

I was honored to begin this deeper relationship with this small group of AO leaders. I still had never met any of them. Even though we continued to work together every single day via our small Advisory email group, I used to chuckle to myself that perhaps they were really a grown-up version of imaginary friends. After all, I hadn't even seen a picture of any one of them. Those were the days of dire warnings about "people you meet online" and about taking great care not to be drawn in by them. And yet here I was, spending every spare moment with these women online (often late into the night, to allow for the different time zones in which we all lived), researching books, dividing up page counts, determining which book was a good fit for which year, matching up our work with Charlotte Mason's own writings, and sharing what was going on in the background with our families and our homeschools. We got to know each other very well.

In the more than twenty years of work on AmblesideOnline, the Advisory has met together in person only eight times. Of those, only five were times when all six of us were present at once.

In the summer of 2005, Lynn Bruce hosted our first AO gathering—a one-day conference in Dallas, Texas. We were very sad that Anne White was unable to come, but the rest of us stayed in Lynn's home, and we talked to Anne by phone. Karen Glass and Leslie Laurio had their youngest daughters with them—just toddlers then. We each spoke at the conference, and God used our various strengths to help those who came and to uplift them as homeschool moms and educators. I sat enthralled as I listened to each of the Advisory members. When it was my turn, I gave a talk designed to encourage by acknowledging hard days but focusing on God's faithfulness to us and the way that our faithfulness in small things yields a harvest. Along with that, I gave a dramatic presentation of Charlotte Mason, which was taken fully from her writings. I had rented a Victorian gown from a theater costume store and had crammed that enormous dress into my small suitcase. I still remember us struggling to iron that monstrosity so that Charlotte would look presentable.

Our curriculum was not only free to use—it was also free to use without registration of any kind. As a result, we have never known just how many families educate their children with AmblesideOnline. So it was something of a shock to me to see how many came to our event and to see the hunger for this beautiful method of educating children. We knew that what we were doing honored the Lord, but this was the first time we saw the results of our work with our own eyes.

When we first got together at Lynn's house, I joked that maybe we would feel more comfortable sitting in front of screens to communicate. But our rapport in person was seamless; it was as though we spoke face-to-face every day. Even against the backdrop of the last-minute preparations for the conference, the excited nervousness of the conference itself, and the wonderful after-party at Lynn's cousin Andrea's house, there were additional treasured moments. We managed to wander around a huge bookstore, eat at a fabulous local restaurant, curl up in comfortable chairs in Lynn's book-lined living room, and all sit at Lynn's dining room table and sing grace together.

But it was five years later in September 2010—over nine years after the work began—when we were finally all in one place in person for the very first time. We met at Wendi's home in Indiana. We took walks to the nearby brook, we ate delicious meals that her daughter Rebecca prepared for us, and we sat and talked and sang and prayed and strategized all day long and into the night.

It was at this get-together at Wendi's in 2010 that we decided we needed some help. The Auxiliary, we would call them. They would help us with the day-to-day workings of all things AO. We discussed the names of younger women whose knowledge of Charlotte Mason was evident, both from their participation in the email list and from their writings on their personal blogs. (We would later use an online forum instead of email for the large AO community, and we also began to moderate several social media platforms). We prayed over and selected several women to ask, and it was not long afterward that the AO Auxiliary was formed: Naomi Goegan, Phyllis Hunsucker, Kathy Livingston, Lani Siciliano, Amy Tuttle, Brandy Vencel, and - for a time - Melisa Hills and Jeanne Webb. Having them as a part of our leadership team has been a gift, their friendship has been a blessing, and their behind-the-scenes work has been a great help to us.

In what was becoming a pattern, it was another five years before we would meet again in person. We had organized an AmblesideOnline two-day retreat, called "At Home with AmblesideOnline," and we on the Advisory and Auxiliary were all going to stay at Wendi's house. This time, though, it was Lynn who could not come, at the last minute. The chemotherapy treatment she was receiving for breast cancer was causing some serious side effects, and she simply could not travel. Lynn's absence was deeply upsetting, both to her and to us. We passed around a tablet one evening so that each of us could say hello to her by video. But of course, it just wasn't the same. Brandy also could not make it, and we were disappointed not to meet her in person. I recall that when we took a group picture, we held up large framed photos of Lynn and Brandy so that they were included.

The 2015 event went well. Cindy Rollins, by now very well known in Charlotte Mason circles, spoke in Lynn's place. It was a joy to get to meet her, and we were honored that she could be with us. Once again, it was shocking to see how far women traveled to attend our little get-together and how hungry they were for what we were able to share with them.

But the retreat was a prelude to a major conference less than a year later. It was going to be the first time we invited guests to come and actually stay on the premises. It was also the first time that every Advisory member and every Auxiliary member was in attendance. We met at a beautiful Christian conference center in Waxahachie, Texas. It was May of 2016. Women came from many different parts of the United States and from all over the world—Canada, Europe, Saudi Arabia, South America, and India. I thought back to Susan Schaeffer Macaulay's statement that Charlotte Mason's ideas could be applied to "a village in India" as Christine, one of our attendees, showed us pictures and told us about a group of women in India who met together regularly to follow AmblesideOnline's curriculum. It was sobering, gratifying, and extremely humbling to the point of awe-inspiring to think that God was using our simple gift of the AO curriculum to bless families in places we would never see.

Some of us also brought our daughters. We had met Lynn's daughters years before in Dallas, along with Leslie's and Karen's toddlers, and we met Wendi's daughters in Indiana. But this was a first, for some Advisory and Auxiliary members, to bring along their daughters to a conference. The girls had the opportunity to fellowship, and they also hopefully gained a better understanding of what their mothers had been doing when all those long hours were spent on the computer.

For me, it was the thrill of a lifetime to have both of my daughters attend this and a later conference. Bethany and Hannah flew to Texas together after I had gone a day or so early to plan and prepare with the others. They told me later what it was like to meet women for the first time who already knew them so well.

"So we got to the parking lot at the conference center and got out of the rental car," Bethany said. "This blonde-haired woman comes out right away, her arms spread wide open, huge smile on her face, and I turned and said to Hannah, 'This has *got* to be Lynn!'" They told me several more delightful stories of their first encounters with the women they'd heard about from me for their entire lives. "When Karen talks, it's like relatable brilliance!"

"Anne is hilarious!" "Leslie has this quiet strength; she looks so happy." "Wendi is amazing. Did you see the glint in her eye?" "Lynn is like a southern version of you!" "I wish I could be a little bit like all of these women!"

That year was made even more special when the Advisory decided to meet in Canada. AmblesideOnline was now AmblesideOnline Educational Foundation (AOEF), and as such, we needed official board meetings. Anne and Wendi were asked to speak at l'HaRMaS, an annual Charlotte Mason retreat held in Kingsville, Ontario. When Karen said she could come from Poland, the rest of us made plans to go to Canada too. This opportunity to get together turned into the long-awaited board meeting. We met in a quaint bed-and-breakfast, a block away from Lake Erie. We had a couple of days together right before l'HaRMaS—just to talk and pray and sing together and to concentrate on AO matters. It was like walking through a dream. I dormed with Anne, and we sat on twin beds in an antique-filled room with a high ceiling and talked into the night. We all took a chilly walk along Lake Erie's shoreline—and mentioned more than once how we had sent children through this very Great Lake by reading Holling Clancy Holling's *Paddle to the Sea*. Later we enjoyed an evening in an eclectic restaurant in town.

Our hostess prepared interesting gourmet meals and always had a selection of individual teapots and teacups for us to use. I have so many other memories: the wide wood planks on the winding staircase, the two different front rooms that we took turns meeting in (depending on the sunlight filtering through), the crocheting projects Wendi and Anne worked on while we talked, the white tablecloth on the dining room table, and the stone fireplace behind us.

We attended the l'HaRMaS conference together. As we went back to our bed-and-breakfast at night, it was as if we all lived close to one another and were just attending a local event. While we were at the conference, the organizers publicly acknowledged our work with AmblesideOnline. It was very moving.

I recall in particular one woman who came and spoke with us during the soup-and-sandwich dinner gathering. She had gone through a difficult crisis in her life, culminating in a time when she traveled to see her dying mother. She had taken her children with her, not knowing how long she would be gone or how to continue homeschooling them during all of this. But she found our HELP plan on the website, and she followed it so she could teach her daughters while far from home. Her mom read aloud to the grandchildren from her hospital bed when she was strong enough, and the memories they made together eased some of the deep pain they later felt when God called her mom (the children's grandma) home to heaven.

HELP (Helping Hand Emergency Lesson Plan) was the minimalist version of AmblesideOnline that we developed in the aftermath of seeing so many people displaced after Hurricane Katrina, which struck the southern coast of the United States in 2005. We tried to imagine a homeschool family whose books and supplies were either destroyed in the hurricane's flooding or left behind as they went to live with relatives. We imagined a family who might be staying in a shelter for a period of time. Our idea was that all they would need was access to a computer or smartphone, and we supplied the rest: full stories (literature, history, nature), maps, math games, folk songs, Bible readings, poems, and even ideas for simple handicrafts.

Over the years, we have learned that families access our HELP plan when other types of storms hit their lives—illness, death of a loved one, job loss, a move, or even other kinds of natural disasters. We have been blessed to know that we were able to provide a little bit of continuity or even sanity during an extremely hard time.

Saying goodbye after our time in Canada was particularly difficult. Wendi would be leaving for the Philippines for a short-term missions trip, and our band of Advisory members would be living in four countries across three continents. Even though our daily contact is through email, the disparate time zones would require another adjustment for how we worked. And we wondered when our next time together would be.

But it was two years later, in July of 2018, that we met in Summerton, South Carolina, for the next board meeting of AOEF. This time Lynn roomed with me, and she was the chef for those delightful days, serving us delicious dishes prepared with love and care and culinary expertise. Once again, the six of us worked diligently on AO's curriculum and on our vision for the future.

In April of 2019, we had the great joy of holding AmblesideOnline Camp Meeting at a place outside of Nashville, Tennessee. Once again, every Auxiliary and Advisory member was there. Kathy, Naomi, Lani, Brandy, Phyllis, and Amy joined Karen, Leslie, Lynn, Anne, Wendi, and me (along with several of our daughters, two of Lani's sons, and Leslie's son Tim) to present the truth and beauty of this educational philosophy. We were all privileged to speak at the event. Rounding out our team of speakers were Sheila Atchley, our long-time friend from the email list years before, and our friends Cindy Rollins, Jeannette Tulis, and Dawn Duran. The preparation took up an entire year, on top of the regular daily AO work. But we got to meet hundreds of women who use AO, and ministering to them brought laughter, tears, and new understanding. Those days were blessed by God, and we were so grateful.

But as important as the times together have been, the sweet fellowship also continues online. We had known even from the very beginning that our relationship as an Advisory was so much more than shared work. We prayed for each other, we supported each other, and we loved each other, through good and bad times. And there were bad times—but not with one another. The grace of God has been poured out upon us; the truth is that we have never argued as an Advisory Board. As someone experienced in leadership teams in churches and other Christian organizations, I can attest to the sad fact that this constant harmony is rare. But it is what has characterized the AO Advisory.

The bad times were things we were going through as individuals or as families. In fact, the collective trials of the members of the AmblesideOnline Advisory—some of which are fairly well-known, others known by just a small circle beyond our group, and some known truly just to one another—have been jarring and shocking, even nearly debilitating at times. We have suffered greatly, and we have gone through some very, very hard things. We have more than once dared to wonder aloud if the work itself made us a target of some kind of spiritual attack.

Our response to these trials, along with supporting one another with love and encouragement, has been prayer. From the earliest days of AO, prayer has been a vital part. We have prayed for all those who use AO, for our supportive Auxiliary and our faithful Moderators, for the children and grandchildren of the Advisory, and for one another. We have set aside Days of Prayer over the years. And we have seen God answer our prayers.

Over twenty years is a long time to work together. We have experienced many firsts: the first of us to graduate a student from homeschool, the first to send a student to college or to see a student into a career, the first to have a son or daughter get married, the first to become a grandmother. There have been hard firsts too, such as the first to lose a parent. And I remember one time thinking, I wonder who will be the first to be widowed.

On August 15, 2020, I knew the answer. My husband collapsed suddenly outside our family cottage on Lake Ontario, our favorite place on earth. Our son Nathan administered CPR until help arrived to take Bill away by ambulance. Bill and our sons had gone ahead earlier that day to do some repairs before the family vacation, but as soon as we got Nathan's anguished call, Bethany and I left home and raced the 300-plus miles from New Jersey. As she drove, I texted my family and my church. And there was no question that the very next ones I needed to reach were the women of my beloved Advisory, to ask them to pray. I texted Lynn, and I later read the posts she sent to the others as they all reacted in real time to the unimaginable events transpiring that afternoon.

While driving north through the mountains of New York state, we learned the news we feared—that Bill had died, likely almost immediately. He was with the Lord. Bill and I had been married thirty-nine and a half years, with four children, two sons-in-law, and three grandchildren. He was sixty-nine years old.

In the excruciating aftermath of that summer day, the Advisory members continued to do what they had always done—to love as Jesus loves, weep with those who weep, and pray for God's grace and strength when both seemed impossible.

The heartache of that year occurred against the backdrop of ongoing illness in our home. The year before Bill died, we had joined with my parents, our oldest son Nathan, and our oldest daughter Bethany and her husband Nate in buying a beautiful home together. With our youngest son Niko and our grandchildren, there were eleven of us in a four-generation household. I homeschooled Niko, and Bethany homeschooled her children. It was a little crazy, but we found spaces for our things and for each other, and we had some happy times.

But two months after we moved in, Bethany's husband Nate was diagnosed with an extremely rare abdominal cancer. Pseudomyxoma Peritonei is said to occur in one in one million people. It was almost as shocking to read of the proposed treatment as it was to learn the diagnosis. They would remove Nate's organs, try to clean them of the cancer, bathe his insides with a heated chemo, and then return what organs they could. This debulking procedure is called the Mother of All Surgeries, and it was scheduled for the fall of 2019.

I remember when the surgeon came out to see Bethany way too soon—only about five hours into what was supposed to take up to twelve. The surgery was not successful. The cancer was too advanced, and even this renowned specialist could not do what he had hoped.

Nate's recovery from that massive operation was hard and slow, but we were together, and we helped one another. My younger daughter Hannah and my son-in-law Jon stayed with us for that first month of Nate's hospitalization, and finally Nate was home. There were many rounds of chemotherapy, and then (although stalled at first by the global pandemic) a very unusual second attempt at debulking was set for May of 2020.

This time, the doctor said it was "95 percent removed" and that we "reset the clock." The AmblesideOnline community, which was already so supportive during the first surgery, had been praying, along with countless others. When I got the good news that afternoon, I felt as though the whole universe had been rocked with joy.

Then after Bill's death that summer, we tried to get life back on track. I took on a little more of the homeschooling as Bethany began to shift her focus toward classes that prepared her for a job in the medical field.

Things got harder. During the winter of 2021, my dad was hospitalized with Covid and then needed much care at home, round the clock at first, which Bethany took over. And although we had rejoiced in what we believed was a miraculous healing, Nate's health began to decline. We got the devastating news that the cancer was growing again.

And on another August day, almost exactly one year after Bill died, God took Nate home to heaven. We were an hour away from leaving for vacation, and there was no warning. Nate was only 35. It was sudden, it was a shock, and it was very hard. The grief was huge, the loss was great, and our hearts were broken.

And a month later, I realized I had not given even a thought to that year's homeschool. Bethany began school full-time, now as a newly widowed single mother planning for her three children's future. The education of her two older girls would be all on me.

I had homeschooled and graduated four children successfully. I had helped with my granddaughters' schooling. I had been a part of the team that created AmblesideOnline. But now I stared at AO's website as if I had never seen it before. I knew my granddaughters had done some of the years already once their adoptions from foster care were finalized and Bethany could direct their education. But they had been through so much, and I wondered how I could take some of what I saw on the screen and use it to heal, to create order, to bring some peace. I thought of so many other families that have come to AO during times of crisis, pain, disruption, and trauma.

I sat at the kitchen table to do that year's planning, beside a long row of schoolbooks lined up along the bay window. The titles would be familiar to AO users: *Ourselves*, *Miracle at Philadelphia*, *Trial and Triumph*, *Answering the Cry for Freedom*, *Book of Marvels*, *George Washington's World*, *Microbe Hunters*, and many more. AO's newly published poetry anthologies were stacked in front of a philodendron, and the prints for picture study were propped up in front of a Christmas cactus.

I stared at the gathered books, art prints, and glowing computer screen, and I was overwhelmed. I didn't feel up to the task. Charlotte Mason's phrase "however imperfectly" characterized my daily endeavors to fix what I could not fix and to heal what I could not heal. How was I to live out the life of Christ before my family? How was I to somehow walk the truth that—as I often say—"God is safe to trust" when my own heart was bruised with events that, despite my best efforts to cling to faith, at times seemed just too much? Charlotte Mason wrote:

> Let us save Christianity for our children by bringing them into allegiance to Christ, the King. How? How did the old Cavaliers bring up sons and daughters, in passionate loyalty and reverence for not too worthy princes? Their own hearts were full of it; their lips spake it, their acts proclaimed it; the style of their clothes, the ring of their voices, the carriage of their heads—all was

> one proclamation of boundless devotion to their king and his cause. (*Home Education,* p. 351)

That is an apt description of the Advisory members as I know them: their own hearts full of devotion to the Savior. That is a description of Charlotte Mason as well. She wrote another six-volume set of her meditations on the Gospel accounts, written completely in poetic form. She loved Jesus Christ. Mason also experienced suffering, most notably in being orphaned as a young girl. She, too, studied educational philosophy and read great books and sought to provide a generous curriculum to the children she knew and loved, and to generations to come. Unlike the rest of us, though, she never became a mother (perhaps another sorrow in her life), and she certainly never saw a computer. But her dedication to the task before her was undergirded by the greatest hallmark of her work, which I believe has been the distinguishing characteristic of ours at AmblesideOnline, and what I realized anew had to be the foundation of my next sacred responsibility.

It is found at the conclusion of volume 1, *Home Education.* In the very last line, after 350 pages of extensive educational principles, philosophical considerations, and practical suggestions, Charlotte Mason refers to a Biblical text and writes simply, "But, once more, 'This kind cometh forth only by prayer'" (Matthew 17:21).

That's it.

That's the last word, the deepest truth, the heart of everything, and it is the path forward, then and now.

This education, this way of life, will come forth, but only by prayer—for AmblesideOnline in the future as it has been in the past, for its countless users all around the world, and for me and my four-generation house, and, this time, "for my grandchildren's sake."

## Another Chapter for Us

That was supposed to be the ending of my part of the book. But then the Advisory entered something we could not have imagined.

In December of 2021, we were talking to each other, as always, about the work of AmblesideOnline and the circumstances of our lives. We were praying for Phyllis, our Auxiliary member in Ukraine, as there was growing concern about what was happening in her country. We were praying for AO families, especially a new one we had just learned about in Kenya. We were working on getting our *Canadian Companion to the AmblesideOnline Poetry Anthology* published, and that was taking up a lot of our time. We were discussing Charlotte Mason's philosophy and our different writing projects. We celebrated Lynn's birthday, shared our plans for Christmas, worried over family members who were sick, and talked about people and places we missed. And we wondered when we could get together in person again.

The day after Christmas, Lynn let us know she was in the hospital. We prayed hard and tried not to worry. Lynn was always brave, always packing so much into her life, and we hated it when anything slowed her down or caused her pain.

Wendi had been quiet, not posting much, but that happened with all of us occasionally, especially during holiday times. And then on New Year's Day, Wendi wrote and asked for prayer: her daughter Angel was very sick and on her way to the emergency room. And Wendi had been sick as well.

There are moments when news comes that stops you where you are, grips a part of your heart, and causes you to pray, instantly. As a grandmother of a special needs grandson, I had often talked with my family about how frightening it would be for our little guy to get seriously ill. And Angel, though an adult, was very much in that category. We had all had the privilege of meeting her, we had heard about her for as long as we had known Wendi, and we knew that even a routine trip to the doctor (or anywhere) was complicated. And now Angel was so sick.

A few days later, we got the frightening news that Wendi, too, was being admitted to the hospital with Covid pneumonia. We began to pray fervently for Wendi. We prayed for her family members by name, we prayed that they would be allowed to be with her and Angel without restrictions, and we prayed for God's mercy. We prayed over every new piece of medical information, every complication, and every update.

We did not know whether Wendi was well enough to read our Advisory messages on her phone. We kept up with words of encouragement for her just in case, and we wrote our fears privately to each other. We wondered when we could tell more people about her condition, to ask them to pray too, but we didn't want to bother the family about that. And then Wendi wrote, "You have my permission to share."

Just hearing from her lifted our spirits. We told her that Jesus was in the room with her and reminded her to hold on, as Lynn said, for a "soon-coming better day." And we told her that we loved her.

We wrote to the AmblesideOnline community on our forum and on our social media platforms. We shared the news about Wendi and Angel, and then we led everyone in prayer:

> Lord Jesus, we are frightened—yet you tell us to fear not. We are worried sick—yet You tell us to cast our every care upon You. We hear what Wendi and Angel are going through in this horrific illness, and we come before You pleading—and You remind us that You are with them. You hear, You answer, You heal.

The response to our prayer request was overwhelming. Hundreds replied with a simple "Praying!" And many others wrote, "I feel like I know her" or "She changed our homeschool." People were praying throughout the United States and around the world.

We learned that at times, Wendi was able to eat or sit in a chair, and the doctor would occasionally express some guarded optimism. And then Wendi's numbers tanked, the news was discouraging, and there was talk of a ventilator. Wendi herself, in what would be her last message to us, asked us to please pray. We continued to express our love, quote the hymns we wished we could sing to her, and pray with fervor.

And right as we were praying for Wendi, we got the news that Anne's beloved father had passed away. All we wanted was to gather around Anne in person, but that was not possible. We gathered virtually around her in love and comfort as we prayed for her and her family in that loss of a parent that Lynn called a "seismic shift." Wendi read our posts about Anne's dad, we later learned, and told one of her daughters that she was so concerned for Anne.

Even after Wendi was intubated, we kept writing to her, telling her of our love and our fervent prayers. We talked to each other, holding each other up. Countless images and sounds of Wendi bombarded our minds—every folk song, every bold fabric, every laugh, every brilliant word. We remembered all her stories about The Cherub, as Angel was called. We knew the stories so well that it was as if we had been present for all those times. We remembered all of us being at her home in Indiana. And we kept saying we weren't ready for even one of us to relocate to a heavenly mansion that didn't have email. We prayed fervently for a miracle.

Wendi continued to decline. We ached for her, for how much she had suffered and was still suffering, and we ached for ourselves, for how much we loved and needed her. We prayed for grace and to be reconciled to God's will, even as we hung onto any glimmer of hope.

On January 20, Angel Capehart went home to heaven.

Lynn wrote, "The Cherub has flown into the arms of Jesus." We knew that God had answered prayer and that Angel was fully healed. But how hard this was for the family, and how hard this would be for Wendi.

Wendi had told us once of a moment when it sounded as though Angel, who never spoke in her life, had sung a couple of recognizable notes of a song. She said it was as though they were on holy ground. Now Angel really was singing. Now she truly was on holy ground.

We waited until after the family had made their announcement, and then we wrote this to the AmblesideOnline community:

> We wish to share with you the news that Angel Capehart, Wendi's daughter, is with the Lord. We prayed for her healing, and God answered, though not in the way we hoped. Angel now is fully whole and singing with the Savior. But the ache she leaves behind cannot be measured. We ask you to continue to pray fervently for Wendi, still on a ventilator, still seriously ill—that God would raise her up and restore her health.

Even in her grief, Wendi's oldest daughter Nicole continued to share medical reports with us, and we continued to express our love to her and the family. Wendi had been on the ventilator for a full week, and although there were small improvements, the big picture was terrifyingly bad.

We prayed, "Lord, we love You, we trust You, we lean on You. But this is really way too much."

We all wanted to be by Wendi's side, to hold her hand, to sing with her, to pray over her, to just sit by her. We could not all go, but Karen could. So we gathered Bible verses Wendi had written in calligraphy or had highlighted on her blogs, and we added the lyrics to hymns that she had treasured or that we had sung together. And Karen printed and took all of that with her in a book of encouragement that could be read to Wendi by anyone who was in the room.

Karen's time with Wendi was precious, deeply moving, and so very hard. Although Wendi was still with us, we knew for certain now that she was slipping away.

A few days later, Nicole told us that the end was very close. The medical staff wanted the family to gather, yet a snowstorm was coming. We prayed for this daunting situation, we prayed for each of them to get there, and we prayed for Wendi, though by this time, our prayers were with few words. Just "Lord Jesus, Lord Jesus! How to be without her?" Yet we knew, beyond anything else we had ever known, that she would be with Christ, that for her it would be, as the Bible says, "far better." We knew that the Gospel story is true, that Jesus is real. We knew Wendi would be happy, whole, and healed in every way. Yet it was hard to hold on to any promise that *we* would be all right.

Late Tuesday afternoon, February 1, 2022, the five of us gathered by video conference. There were too few squares on the screen, we noted. Five was not enough. Our familiar faces were framed against familiar backgrounds, but this sacred space was brand new. We had never gone this way before. We gathered to be together, to walk Wendi home in our own way, to pray for her as the veil grew so thin, and to pray for her family.

Before long, we received the message from Nicole that her dear Mom, our beloved Wendi, had left this earth. Wendi was with Jesus.

We hold to ourselves what took place in those hours before and after that message. But we can share this: we prayed, we cried, and we sang. Actually, it was Lynn who sang. In her beautiful mezzo-soprano voice, she began the hymn "How Firm a Foundation." And in the very start of our fresh grief, her singing reminded us of these promises:

> Fear not, I am with thee, O be not dismayed,
> For I am thy God, I will still give thee aid;
> I'll strengthen thee, help thee, and cause thee to stand,
> Upheld by My righteous, omnipotent hand.
>
> When through the deep waters I call thee to go,
> The rivers of sorrow will not overflow;
> For I will be with thee, thy troubles to bless,

And sanctify to thee thy deepest distress.

And even now, we can recall her singing these words:

The soul that on Jesus hath leaned for repose,
I will not, I will not desert to his foes;
That soul, though all hell should endeavor to shake,
I'll never, no never, no never forsake!

We had already painstakingly prepared how we would announce Wendi's death to the AmblesideOnline community. Once the family made their announcements, we posted ours:

> It is with the deepest sorrow that we must share with you the difficult news that our beloved friend, colleague, and sister, Wendi Capehart, is with the Lord. She was released from her sickness-ridden body tonight in the presence of her children, and she was immediately with the Savior who loves her with an everlasting love. We ask that you pray for Wendi's entire family, still grieving the loss of Angel on January 20. We ask that you pray for us, as we seek to reconcile ourselves to that which cannot be reconciled, this side of Glory. Precious in the sight of the Lord is the death of His saints. To be absent from the body is to be present with the Lord. We grieve, not as those who have no hope. Until that day when we see you again, we love you, Wendi, more than words can say. We will be remembering her as an AO community more fully in the coming days. We wish to reassure you that the work of AmblesideOnline, which (after the raising of her children) was Wendi's other life work, will go on, though the loss of Wendi's knowledge, brilliance, and compassion can never, ever be replaced.

The very next day, Lynn went in for extensive cancer scans. The fragility of life was fresh in our minds as once again we prayed throughout her time at the hospital.

Karen and I were able to attend the memorial service in Indiana for Wendi and Angel. Another snowstorm nearly derailed my opportunity, but despite an overnight delay, my flight made it in time to get to the church. We met with three other friends, and we felt honored to be able to sit with Wendi's loved ones for that precious afternoon of remembering her and Angel's extraordinary lives.

In the meantime, Lynn got her results back, and the news was not good. The cancer had spread to her liver.

I remember where I was when she first told us about being diagnosed with breast cancer. It was in August of 2007, and I was in a hotel in Chicago, about to get ready for my nephew's wedding. I remember that I was sitting on the floor quickly checking email, with my laptop propped open on a chair. I remember it almost like a photograph, frozen in time. Yet in that life-changing moment, Lynn led us with the confidence that she was in God's hands, and she reassured us that God would see her through. And He did—beyond what we could imagine.

Over and over again, God brought Lynn through. When the cancer metastasized and was found in her bones, God brought her through. When she endured surgery after surgery, God brought her through. When treatment after treatment worked, then failed, and new experimental ones were tried, when she dealt with the indignities of cancer and when she endured the losses, God brought her through. She talked to us about all of it. We were, I believe, her safe place, as we all were for each other. And we prayed without ceasing, for years.

That continued to be a hard year for Lynn, physically. She kept up with the work of AmblesideOnline, and she still told us about her time with her family and their wonderful adventures. But there was a shift. I didn't want to believe it; in fact, I kept telling myself that God had brought her through so many times before, He would do it again. I always told her she did everything, as was said of dancer Ginger Rogers, "backwards and in high heels," and that had not changed. She was remarkable, always. We just wanted *always* to continue.

That fall, the "seismic shift" of the loss of a parent happened to me this time. My beloved Dad—who had been my pastor throughout my entire life, who brought me to work alongside him in ministry, who cheered me on in every endeavor, who was my friend and above all my hero—went to be with Jesus. During those last nights in our home when Dad was under hospice care, I sat beside his bed in the dim light. And after sending texts to update my family, I always wrote to the Advisory. They were there to help me, to encourage me in Dad's last hours, to remind me of their prayers and their love during yet another deep heartache. And on the very day when Dad was scheduled to lead a Bible study in our home, my brother Chuck and I spoke at his funeral. "I thank my God upon every remembrance of you," I said at the end. Even then, I had a preview of what the following days would be like because of my Advisory friends who had walked that hard path ahead of me. I recall Lynn telling us that after her own preacher-dad's burial, she had said, "I don't know how to do this next part." Suddenly I understood that.

In January of 2023, I learned that my daughter Bethany would have a week off from nursing school in mid-March. Her break would make it easier for me to get away. I asked the Advisory: Could this finally work after almost four years? Could we get together? We could meet in Dallas, where Lynn lived, so she would not have to travel. She had been back in the hospital in December, and since then she had been quieter, but we knew all her energy had to be for her family. Then despite how she was feeling, she was the one who directed our plans. She told us of dreams she had long had for us—to walk together in the Dallas Arboretum for the annual "Dallas Blooms" tulip display, she told us of the restaurant where we would eat, and she picked out the place where we would stay. Because of her health, she said it was daunting to imagine, but she wrote optimistically, "God knows March and I don't."

We reached the one-year anniversary of Wendi's death. In so many ways, it often seemed as though Wendi would write to us again—that it would just have been a long absence and that all would be well. But of course, that was our grief talking. We knew she was gone, and we knew where she was. We continued to pray for her family, and we continued to pray for ourselves and our work. For even in the increasing worry for Lynn and the ongoing loss of Wendi, we kept on working. At times it was a distraction. We finished a project for our Bible schedule that Wendi had begun, we created a page of resources for Easter, and we kept up with our daily set of tasks for AmblesideOnline. But all the while, we worried about how Lynn was doing.

Then her daughter Caitlin wrote to us, and we learned that Lynn was back in the hospital. She wasn't doing well. There was still hope: another new drug for her type of cancer had just been approved by the Food and Drug Administration. But we had walked with her for many years, and we knew this was very serious. We knew she had to get stronger, even for new treatment. We prayed for her doctor by name, for each of her family members, and for her—that God would give her comfort, clarity, a sense of His presence, and healing. "Mercy, courage, grace," she always said.

We kept on praying; we kept on "plowing in hope," as Lynn so often reminded us from the Scriptures.

On February 13, Lynn entered the intensive care unit of the hospital. It was as though we had run out of words. Many times, a prayer of "Please, God," was all we had. Other times, we wrote our pain to each other, and we prayed.

> Lord Jesus, every breath is yours. Help her tonight. How we want her here. How we want to see her and be with her. Jesus, we know she's suffered so very long. Lord, please help us, and oh, Jesus, help her. We are shattered. Again, Lord? Again? Steady us. Thank You for this gift

> of friendship—beyond what we could even dream of. Hold us all so close in Your everlasting arms.

Our hearts were once again in a hospital room far away. We followed the family's lead, and once they made her condition public, we asked for prayer from the AmblesideOnline community. Many families sent cards, and many others wrote online that they were praying for her.

Lynn's cousin Andrea texted me and asked if I was available to speak to Lynn. She would put the phone on speaker and hold it to Lynn's ear. As I waited for Andrea's call, I prayed— "Lord, give me the words, and please, help me not to cry." I had this fear I would break down, and that was not what I wanted to do.

That treasured five-minute call on behalf of all of us ended with the word I had never, ever wanted to say to her: goodbye.

The next day, Lynn moved into hospice care. And on February 18, 2023, Lynn Bruce was ushered into the presence of God.

The four of us, on our computers, sat together, although across many miles. We had talked about death before. Lynn had, in fact, spoken to us about her own death. But all the conversations in the world were inadequate for the actual loss of each of these loved ones and now for Lynn. I remembered Lynn's words that hard times would "come to pass. Now is not forever. The darkness will end." In remembering that, she was turning us toward Jesus still.

Once again, we went through the painful task of lovingly preparing something we hoped would come close to honoring Lynn. Once again, we waited on the family, and then we posted this to our AO community:

> With shattered hearts yet with full confidence in the truth of the Gospel message, we must announce the difficult news that our beloved friend, colleague, and sister on the AmblesideOnline Advisory, Lynn Bruce, is now with the Lord she loved so well. Lynn's fifteen-and-a-half-year battle with advanced metastatic breast cancer ended

> today, February 18, in the presence of her loving family. Lynn was immediately ushered into the presence of Jesus Christ, who has loved her with an everlasting love.

We listed all the members of Lynn's family, asked for prayer for each of them, and then wrote:

> And we ask, once again, that you pray for us, as we seek to reconcile ourselves to that which cannot be reconciled, this side of Glory. Precious in the sight of the Lord is the death of His saints. To be absent from the body is to be present with the Lord. We grieve deeply, yet not as those who have no hope. After our beloved Advisory sister Wendi Capehart went to heaven a year ago, Lynn took on the task of finishing the final year's selection of folk songs. The song Lynn scheduled for this month, "Wayfaring Stranger," ends with these words: "I'm going there to meet my Saviour, To sing His praise forevermore. I'm only going over Jordan, I'm only going over home." We will be remembering Lynn as an AO community more fully in the coming days. We wish, again, to reassure you that the ministry of AmblesideOnline, which (after the raising of her children) was Lynn's other life work, belongs to God. She reminded us often of that great truth. AmblesideOnline will continue, undergirded by the magnificent legacy of Lynn's word artistry, her foundational knowledge in Charlotte Mason philosophy, and her enduring vision of God's faithfulness. Until that day when we see you again, we love you, Lynn, more than words can say.

During the next couple of days, Karen and I made plans to attend Lynn's funeral in Dallas. I had packed a small bag, intending to go straight from the plane to the service. Then the day before my early morning flight, my son Nathan was suddenly quite sick.

And by that evening, my granddaughter was sick. I was concerned for them, while thinking, "This cannot be happening." And in the middle of the night, an hour before I was to leave for the airport, I, too, got very sick. I crawled back into bed, feeling crushed.

We knew the funeral would be live-streamed, so later that day, Karen, Leslie, Anne, and I all gathered together on a video conference. It was startling this time to see that we took up only four squares on the screen. We each watched the funeral itself on separate devices. We watched the singing, the Scripture reading, the message by Lynn's dear brother—all of it. It was Christ-honoring and full of remembrances of Lynn's remarkable life.

One month later, we met in Dallas. The four of us stayed at the place Lynn had selected for us to stay. We went to see "Dallas Blooms" at the Arboretum and walked beside half a million splashes of color. We ate at the Mediterranean restaurant she had chosen for us. We continued with AO work, though that part was not her plan. She had wanted us to use this time as a retreat, remembering Wendi and healing together. But we needed to do some work in person, to remind ourselves that the work we had begun would continue in the strength of the Lord.

And we had one more place to go. Lynn hadn't put it on the itinerary for this trip, but she had talked to us about it so often in the past. We always knew it was another dream of hers for us to go to the farm.

It was an afternoon we will never forget. The farm was where Lynn grew up, and she had told us so much about it that the sight of it seemed familiar. It is now the home of Lynn's daughter Caitlin, Caitlin's husband Dan, and their four young children. We met many of the members of Lynn's family that day, and thanks to their gracious hospitality, we talked, we laughed, we ate, and we shared stories about this woman we loved so much. And later, under the wide Texas sky, the four of us walked silently down the driveway, across the road, and over the cattle guard, Karen carrying the bouquet of white tulips we had brought for Lynn's grave.

We walked on the long dirt entrance that led all the way up to the church, and then we stepped into that sacred space where Lynn learned of Jesus from her Daddy's pulpit. Caitlin met us there, and she led us out to the cemetery where Lynn was laid to rest. Those moments are just too precious and personal to describe.

The next morning, we were packed up and ready to leave for the airport. We sat one more time in front of the fireplace and took some time to sing. The six of us had sung together in so many places: in Lynn's and Wendi's homes, in the house by the lake in South Carolina, at the bed-and-breakfast in Canada, with hundreds of women at our conferences and at AmblesideOnline Camp Meeting. We had even sung together in an airport once. This time, in the little house picked out for us, I kept hearing Wendi's and Lynn's voices filling in the parts, and I struggled to sing. Soon we went to the airport and hugged goodbye. We would be writing to each other by that night, carrying on as we had for so many years.

The next Sunday, I headed to church. It has been strange to attend a new place where my Dad isn't the preacher, but I'm grateful for the witness of Calvary Chapel of North Jersey. It's quite a distance from my house, and I could see the New York City skyline when I drove up to find a parking spot. As I walked into the sanctuary to sit with my family, the worship music had already begun. That morning it included the hymn "Great is Thy Faithfulness." How often we had sung that hymn together as Advisory members or at our AmblesideOnline conferences. It has become a kind of anthem for us. Despite tears, I found my voice this time:

> ...Strength for today, and bright hope for tomorrow,
> Blessings all mine, with ten thousand beside.
> Great is Thy faithfulness! Great is Thy faithfulness!
> Morning by morning, new mercies I see;
> All I have needed Thy hand hath provided;
> Great is Thy faithfulness, Lord, unto me.

It was true. He had been faithful. Even in the trials, even in the losses, we were not left without His care, His mercy, His strength, and His hope. And AmblesideOnline has been God's work, covered by prayer from the start. It was the six of us who had been given the gift of an extraordinary friendship and the opportunity to create AmblesideOnline. And by His grace, He will still use all of us to tell our story and to share our heart. And someday, as He promised, there will be a great reunion.

*Strength for today, and bright hope for tomorrow.*

## Leslie: The Idea That Became AmblesideOnline

> What is an Idea? "A living thing of the mind," according to past philosophers from Plato to Bacon to Coleridge. We say that an idea strikes us, or impresses us, or seizes us, or takes possession of us, or rules us. As it turns out, our common terms are closer to the truth than the conscious thought being expressed, which is usually the case. It's no exaggeration to credit this kind of action and power to an idea. We form an ideal—which is to say, an embodied idea—and our ideal exerts the strongest formative influence on us. Why do you devote yourself to a particular pursuit or cause? "Because, twenty years ago, such and such an idea struck me," is a common response to every kind of life with purpose, every life devoted to working out a particular idea. (*Parents and Children in Modern English*, pp. 33–39)

> Ideas are living and have the ability to inspire. (*School Education in Modern English*, p. 134)

My role with AmblesideOnline has been coming up with recklessly ambitious ideas and then pestering people to help put them into action. Eventually I ended up as webmaster, not because I had any technical experience but because everyone else was busy actually sifting through books and making curriculum decisions and I was the only one with the time to learn how to do it.

I started homeschooling in 1996, when my first child was six. I had intended on doing Charlotte Mason, but when my son started first grade, I realized I had some vague ideas about Charlotte Mason but no definite guidelines about how to actually *do* it. It wasn't until we got our first computer in 1998 that I found a community of C.M. moms online where I could ask questions and get some specifics.

Back in 1998, the landscape was completely different than it is now. I wasn't unusual in getting my first computer; lots of people still didn't own computers. Project Gutenberg had some books, but nothing like they have now. Archive.org, another source of e-books, had just gotten off the ground and was still pretty much unknown. YouTube, Librivox, Google, Facebook, and Paypal didn't exist. Music files online were usually in MIDI format. Amazon existed, but not many people bought books there; most people bought books at homeschool conventions or ordered from catalogues like Christian Book Distributors or specialty companies like Timberdoodle that catered to homeschoolers. Cell phones weren't a thing, although some enterprising businesspeople had car phones, and PDAs (precursors to cell phones) were beginning to trend among them as well. Back in the Stone Age of the internet, we used Lycos, AltaVista, AskJeeves, and Dogpile to search for information. Online communities used email groups (or email loops) through list servers that predated Yahoo, and people with a body of information to share publicly used free websites like GeoCities.

Once I had a computer with internet access, I spent a lot of time reading articles online about classical education by the Bluedorns of Trivium Pursuit, unschooling on MidnightBeach.com, and Charlotte Mason on Lynn Hocraffer's GeoCities website. Through Lynn Hocraffer, I found the cmason email list, and that was the turning point in my homeschool journey. Lynn would post detailed and scholarly articles to teach us about the C.M. method, and Cindy Rushton would post inspiring articles to make us feel like C.M. wasn't impossible and to encourage us that we could *do it*!

Very few moms in the group had read the Charlotte Mason series—the set was fairly expensive and had to be ordered by mail from Christian Book Distributors unless you were lucky enough to attend a homeschooling convention and find it being sold there. And even if you owned the books, they were written in Victorian prose that was difficult for moms with a public-school education to fully understand. Many had read *For the Children's Sake* by Susan Schaeffer Macaulay, *A Charlotte Mason Education* by Catherine Levison, or *The Charlotte Mason Study Guide* by Penny Gardner. Karen Andreola was publishing quarterly magazines with her own writings about the C.M. method, some vintage *Parents' Review* articles, and letters to the editor, and those were very helpful. Her *Charlotte Mason Companion* hadn't been published yet. There were some moms in the email group who had read the first of Charlotte Mason's books (*Home Education*), and they felt like experts to me.

*Parents' Review* articles from Charlotte Mason's magazine were available only if you contacted the Armitt Museum in England and purchased photocopies of individual articles (but first you'd have to purchase photocopies of the tables of contents and then hope you guessed right about what an article might be about based on its title) or else by going to the Library of Congress in Washington, D.C., and photocopying them yourself. Thus, many of us were getting our C.M. information secondhand—often from moms who were familiar with only *Home Education*, which is for children aged nine and under. There were lots of misconceptions going around about the Charlotte Mason method that made it sound like unschooling—it was considered gentle, undemanding, child-led, not something you'd do past sixth grade. The image I had of Charlotte Mason was leisurely outdoor walks with a mysterious thing called a nature notebook, daily tea with a floral teapot and lace tablecloth, lovely vintage books of poetry and classic novels, and math taught with beads or seashells. This all sounded lovely, but I had three little boys, and none of this seemed to apply to boys, or to older students either. Most C.M. moms seemed to be putting their kids in public school once they reached high school. The few who continued homeschooling through high school tended to shift to classical education—which also consisted mostly of homeschool moms trying to figure things out as they went. Classical schools and co-ops we are now familiar with as household names weren't around then. Audiobooks meant going to the library and borrowing cassette tapes or CDs, and podcasts didn't exist.

The cmason email group became my support group, my source of education, and my place to find resources and practical suggestions. We were all still learning about C.M., still making discoveries: "Look at this! Charlotte Mason was teaching Latin *and* another foreign language!" "'Living books' doesn't always mean historical fiction stories that are fun for my children—there's more to it than that." "I've read through *Home Education*, and daily teatime, while a lovely British tradition, isn't ever mentioned as a C.M. practice." "Did you know that C.M. actually did some long and strenuous hikes? Maybe we should be picturing her in hiking boots rather than lace and frills!" There was a wonderful feeling of camaraderie—freely sharing new information with the group to expand the understanding of the C.M. method, letting others know about resources that could be used in a C.M. way, posting a link to an e-book that was newly available online, or typing out and sending a classic poem others could share with their children, helping other moms in an atmosphere of encouragement and generosity.

But after a few months on the group, among the various book suggestions I saw some confusion about which children's books are necessary and promote C.M. principles and which are enjoyable but not necessarily must-reads or living books. There are lots and lots of good books, but which books are truly great books that should be included in every child's experience? Which ones stretch children's mental muscles and expand their perspective so that they're able to move up to the Great Books later?

## I'm Formulating a Plan...

In a July 1999 email to one of the moms I most admired on the email group, Karen Glass, I suggested, "I'm formulating a plan.... Why don't we make up a list of C.M. must-reads using only the cream of the crop of the books from other lists and books we know of, and make the list say something like 'These are C.M.-type books that should not be missing from a child's education; these are the books that we feel are necessary to build up a child's mind in preparation to read the 100 Great Books. The gaps can be filled in with lighter, wholesome reading from the many various other homeschool booklists.'"

Karen's response: "Has anyone ever told you, you are an ambitious person?"

We recruited another mom from the CMSeries email group to help us weed through the various booklists posted for homeschoolers and books that listed which books to read your children. In August 1999, we ended up with a list of 120 books a child should read before the age of twelve to be prepared for the harder books that would be standard in a classical education (because it was assumed that high school students would "graduate" to a Great Books classical education after their C.M. education). The list wasn't divided into age groups, and an *X* denoted books that could be found online, although no links were provided. It included *Peter Pan*, *Little Women*, and *Pilgrim's Progress*, as well as the vague "Poetry of William Wordsworth" with no book title or suggested poems.

## Can't This Be Streamlined Somehow?

I also saw the same questions being asked by new moms in the email group: "What living history book should I use?" "How do I teach early math?" "Are there any C.M.-friendly foreign language programs?" These kinds of practical, immediate concerns seemed to drown out questions about C.M. principles and ideas and how to actually *do* a Charlotte Mason style of education. There were lots of moms on the list, and it seemed like every one of them was struggling to understand the C.M. method while trying to create her own C.M. curriculum at the same time. It was like each of us was trying to reinvent the wheel and looking to one another for tips. Surely it would be easier if there was a way to streamline the process of transferring the most basic information on some kind of web page where these things could be listed and referred to. After all, the same resources were usually being suggested: *A Child's History of the World* by Virgil Hillyer for early history, David Quine's Cornerstone Curriculum for early math, Charles and Mary Lamb's *Tales from Shakespeare*, Anna Botsford Comstock's *Handbook of Nature Study*. Rather than have new moms join the group and ask for these resources, wouldn't it be handy to have it all compiled in one place? That way, the group could focus on learning how to use those resources in a C.M. context.

A local friend of mine, Jackie Fulop, was reading the Series and wanted to start a new group focused on the more philosophical aspect of Charlotte Mason—about the whys of what she recommended, so I helped her get the group set up and joined it to listen in and hopefully learn something, although much of the group discussion was over my head.

## If You Post It, They Will Come

I was loving what I was hearing about the Charlotte Mason method. It was so freeing and effective, and it treated children with such respect that I was convinced if we made a clear explanation of the method freely and easily accessible, everyone would want to teach their children with these methods. We just needed to come up with a concise explanation that would make everyone want to do C.M. That seemed simple and obvious enough. So as a group project on the CMSeries email group, we compiled a clear-cut explanation of what defined the C.M. method in order to separate vague misconceptions from accurate facts. Our list included narration, copywork, nature, habits, living books, short lessons. It did *not* include teatime, Victorian illustrations, or a vague definition of a living book as "any book my child likes." We came up with a list of eighteen items that we felt were the defining aspects of a true C.M. education titled "What is C.M.?" that is now posted on the AO website. We hoped that would clarify the method for new moms while also encouraging them to want to know more and read Charlotte Mason's books for themselves to flesh out the details.

Explaining the C.M. method simply and concisely, yet comprehensively and accurately, has always been an intriguing puzzle to me. Some years later, while waiting for a child at a piano lesson, I thought it might be fun to see if I could take the definitives of a C.M. education and boil the method down to less than a hundred words. I was almost successful—I got down to 101 words:

> In a Charlotte Mason education, the child's dignity as an individual made in God's image is respected. His education connects him to the world around him, building relationships with God and people from various places and times. Outdoor life is emphasized. Focused attention at short lessons keeps the mind fresh and leaves free time for personal interests. Living books put the child in touch with vital ideas, and narration teaches him to process those ideas. Copywork and dictation are the bulk of language arts instruction. The educational course of study is teacher-directed, but learning is the responsibility of the student.

## I Have an Idea...

But this project got me thinking. What if a mom who was new to Charlotte Mason did not have to reinvent the wheel by trying to discover what we had already learned nor have to ask what to use for different subjects in order to put together her own curriculum before she really had a grasp of the approach? What if we could make it easier for her by having our list of what defines a Charlotte Mason education as well as a ready-made collection of resources to implement it? Imagine how freeing it would be to have all the necessary information, links, and support so she could easily put together her own materials and then dive in and start schooling! She wouldn't need to write her own curriculum but instead would be able to focus on understanding the hows and whys of Charlotte Mason.

We already had the foundation of a booklist with the list of 120 books we had posted. All it needed was to be split into grade levels and have links added to access the texts online. We could suggest things like poets, composers, and artists that moms could refer to, even if the only culture they were familiar with was Robert Frost, Beethoven, and Monet. We could link artists to an online collection of paintings and suggest affordable CDs of classical music. We could recommend C.M.-friendly math resources and foreign language programs. Imagine making a C.M. living education accessible to any homeschooler with internet access. Every child in the world could have this kind of education almost free! Sounds simple enough, right?

I wrote an email to one of the groups in the fall of 1999:

> It would be nice for moms to be able to find, all in one place, most of what they need to start teaching a C.M. education, starting with the booklist, the FAQ about what makes a Charlotte Mason education, some poetry online, and access to hard-to-find books with the use of

> e-texts, maybe some kind of a guide to teaching music and art. It sure would be nice for moms not to have to start from scratch and build their own curriculums like I think most of us probably did through trial and error. Just think, if classical music MIDI sites and art sites were included, and links to C.M.-friendly math programs like Math-U-See and Making Math Meaningful…there could actually be a free Charlotte Mason curriculum online!

And thus the idea of a free online C.M. curriculum began. It was quite an ambitious project for a mom who was still working her way through the Series! But I recruited a couple of smart C.M. moms I knew online and persuaded them that the world needed a C.M. curriculum, and they agreed to help. The three of us approached the project with different priorities. I was really intrigued with the idea of making a great education available free to anyone in any financial situation, and the other two were more focused on making sure every book and every resource met Charlotte Mason's standard for quality. One mom was also interested in finding books that her kids would actually read. In the end, we decided that in each subject, we would use the best book that was either online free or widely available and affordable so that any mom would be able to get the books.

The first step was to divide the booklist we had already compiled into subjects. It was immediately apparent that we had plenty of fairy tales, mythology, historical fiction, nature tales (mostly about animals), and literature—but hardly any real history, no actual science, and no geography. It wasn't much of a foundation for a full, well-rounded curriculum. The history books we wanted to use (*An Island Story* and *This Country of Ours* by H.E. Marshall, *Colonial Children* and *Camps and Firesides of the Revolution* by Albert Bushnell Hart, *A History of the United States and Its People* by Edward Eggleston) were out of print and not available online. We discussed finding copies of these books and typing them ourselves to post online.

We decided to ask Karen Glass to look at our list to see if we were on the right track. We were surprised and delighted that she was actually interested in helping us! Her first comment was that we had way too many books listed and we'd need to pare it down to meet C.M.'s standards of going slowly through a few books. Over the next couple of weeks, we worked like mad to get the project done. We set a deadline of November 12, 1999 for ourselves because one mom wanted to start schooling then. We compared what Charlotte Mason had done, based on the few schedules we had from her PNEU schools, to determine how many books should be scheduled in each term (What? Only three literature books?) and how many pages should be read for each grade. We considered whether we should arrange the school year into quarters and semesters or twelve-week terms. After a lot of thinking, we decided on twelve-week terms, partly because we preferred doing three artists and composers a year rather than two (one per semester) or four (one per quarter), partly because it was more flexible and easier for year-round schoolers to add a term over the summer, and partly because it's what Charlotte Mason was using. We solved the problem of having to limit our scheduled must-read literature selections by adding a "Free Reading" category. It took lots of hours at the computer, lots of emails back and forth, and lots of late nights (and, for me in my pre-sugarfree life, lots of Tootsie Rolls!), but it was finally ready! We picked an artist (Albrecht Dürer) and a composer (Beethoven) off the top of our heads and figured we could work out a master plan for that part of the curriculum later. We knew it wasn't really finished yet, but it was at a point where we could actually start trying it. And we could refine it as we went, adding things like an art list and specific poems and making book substitutions if our children couldn't handle the ones we were using.

And with that, the first incarnation of AO was unveiled, but with a different name: Parents' Union Online (PUO). The name "Parents' Union" reflected our vision for this project. The idea was to start with a basic framework, and parents using it would add links and other resources as they found them for the benefit of other parents to expand the project—a "moms helping moms" venture for the good of the world's children, with no thought of buying or selling or making a profit. This would not be a business but a resource for the education and raising of the next generation.

The curriculum list only covered grades 1–6, at which time we assumed parents could slide into classical education if they continued to homeschool. There was no weekly schedule—only a list of books, art, classical music, and poetry for the term.

We thought it might be fun to invite anyone who was interested to test it with us and to give us feedback and suggest changes as they figured out what was working and what wasn't with their students. We started a support group on an email list run on Onelist (before people were using Yahoo). We were surprised at the number of people who wanted to test this thing with us, especially considering that it wasn't really done yet! And, based on critical feedback that displayed an understanding of C.M. methods, we asked Jackie Fulop, Anne White, and Leslie Smith to join us.

## Can the Charlotte Mason Series Be Made Available to Every Mom?

Another need I observed was for moms to go to the source and read the books Charlotte Mason wrote. Most of our time and focus in those first few years was spent in convincing moms to read the Series for themselves and explaining that the Charlotte Mason method was more structured than people thought. Too often, moms tended to do a version of child-led unschooling with a few elements of Charlotte Mason thrown in and thought they were doing a proper Charlotte Mason education. In an effort to make the Series available to more C.M. moms, we decided to type up the volumes, which were old enough to be in the public domain, and post them online. This project took three or four years, as the text had to be manually typed by multiple volunteers and there were six books. With the text available online, any mom could go right to the source and learn for herself about the C.M. method firsthand. Now anyone with a computer could read and search the Series!

## Building on the Idea

As our PUO curriculum gained steam, we started thinking of ways to make C.M. homeschooling even easier for parents. What if we could save parents the experience of being in the middle of a Shakespeare play, only to find that the content wasn't suitable for children, by having family-appropriate plays prescheduled for each term? What if we scheduled Plutarch's *Lives* right into the curriculum rather than leaving it as an afterthought, likely to be left out? What if we could compile a web page of poetry for each term and save parents the hassle of going through reams of poetry to find the poems by the term's poet that are suitable for children? What if we divided the term's books into weekly readings to help parents with pacing? How about specifying an area of nature study for each term to make one less decision for a parent to have to consider?

And then we started thinking—what if we continued past sixth grade? A group of moms who were already using the curriculum for their younger children formed a group and started work on Year 7, headed by Wendi Capehart, who had children who were already doing C.M. past sixth grade, and using notes from Donna-Jean Breckenridge, who had outlined a C.M. high school plan for her daughter. With Wendi came the addition of folk songs and hymns, something that had never been formally part of a modern C.M. curriculum.

By mid-2001, over 400 moms had subscribed to our email support group. We had a change of leadership as one of the founding moms left, and Donna-Jean Breckenridge and Lynn Bruce joined—the final members of the Advisory team. We also changed the name from Parents' Union Online to AmblesideOnline, named for the area where Charlotte Mason lived and worked. The AO that exists today was officially born on July 4, 2001.

## An Easier, Quicker Version of the C.M. Series

All six of Charlotte Mason's vintage books were posted online so that any mom who wanted to read the Series could have access to them. But for some moms (like myself!), Charlotte Mason's antiquated language was a barrier. I started summarizing each paragraph as I read volume 1, *Home Education*, and posting my summaries to the CMSeries group for those who might be having a difficult time understanding the text. That exercise was a huge help to me personally. It forced me to stop, figure out exactly what Charlotte Mason was saying, and then summarize it in my own words—a bit like narration. So I continued this with all six books. Eventually, these summaries were compiled and posted on the AO website with the goals of making it possible for moms in every stage in their own education to grasp the ideas that Charlotte Mason spent her life writing about and of helping them see that there was much, much more to a Charlotte Mason education than nature walks, narration, and storybooks. It's a whole package, and every aspect, every detail works together to awaken a child's mind.

This also meant that I finally read all six books in the Series.

## Continued Growth and a Paraphrase

As the project continued to grow, the original vision of providing C.M. information and a curriculum guide for parents to use or adjust at no cost continued to be the driving force of the project. By the end of 2001, 800 moms were subscribed to the email group.

Anne started creating study guides to help families read Plutarch, the high school years began to take shape, and we focused on refining the curriculum.

Since summarizing the Series had been such a help to my understanding of Charlotte Mason and since I was often holding a sleeping baby and mostly only able to do computer work, I decided to see if I could rephrase volume 1, a sentence at a time, using different words than Charlotte Mason had used but making it clear enough for a child (or distracted mom) to understand. By the baby's fourth birthday, all six volumes were paraphrased and posted online. I hoped this would remove the language barrier that discouraged so many C.M. parents from reading her books. Now we had made the C.M. series available in the original Victorian prose (which began to collect our annotations), in a summary for quick skimming, and in an easy-to-read modern paraphrase. There was no reason why any and every aspiring Charlotte Mason mom couldn't get a full picture of this method of educating, even if she wasn't in a position to order the Series and even if she couldn't understand the wordy Victorian style of writing.

In July 2005, we had our first-ever AO Conference in Dallas, Texas. Karen and I both brought our toddlers. About 150 people attended. This was the first time most of the Advisory had ever met face to face; we had put the AO project together virtually, via emails, for all those years.

## More Changes

Meanwhile, the homeschool movement grew, and so did interest in Charlotte Mason. More and more families used AmblesideOnline. This meant our email group grew, and our list of projects and improvements to the curriculum kept expanding. We wanted to overhaul the science part of the curriculum, add AO exams, and make the website easier to navigate. In September 2010, the Advisory met in Indiana to discuss all of these ideas.

We talked about adding some newer moms with younger children to our team as an Auxiliary group to assist us and to help us understand the needs of younger moms. After all, the homeschool community had changed in the ten years since we had started the AO project. We were all graduating students, while younger moms had children just beginning Year 1.

When we were getting started, homeschoolers tended to be pioneering mavericks, fighting for their right to homeschool and determined to turn over every stone to seek out resources and turn their students into independent and resourceful readers in a world that didn't make it easy to homeschool. By 2010, homeschoolers had become a profitable market, and lots of options were available to them. Newer homeschoolers no longer had to search high and low for resources, or create their own educational plans, or prove that homeschooling could be done. The internet had changed too. Though our vision of making Charlotte Mason education doable for anyone hadn't changed, we found that we needed to have a cleaner, less cluttered website. We also needed to have more helps readily available: things like weekly schedules in a grid format, lengthy notes about books moved to a footnote section at the bottom of the page for a less cluttered look, and selected portions from public domain texts already compiled and ready to print. Foreign language programs we had recommended ten years earlier no longer existed, and new ones had been created. New math programs like Math-U-See, Right Start, and Teaching Textbooks had become more popular with C.M. parents than the programs parents used to recommend ten years earlier.

In 2012 we moved our support group from an email list to an online forum. The newer crop of homeschooling parents tended to look for support on Facebook, so we also opened a group there.

When Year 12 was posted in 2013, the AmblesideOnline curriculum was complete. We began to focus on filling some gaps, such as writing a paraphrased version of *Parables from Nature*—originally for my daughter, who was having a hard time with the original, but posted online to help other families who were giving up on these wonderful stories because they were too difficult for their children. Anne White continued writing more Plutarch's *Lives* study guides and refined their format. In 2016, we officially became the AmblesideOnline Educational Foundation.

## Can't We Make This Easier for Co-ops?

We began hearing from parents who wanted to do a Charlotte Mason style of education but were involved in a classical cooperative because there were no other options unless they wanted to homeschool in isolation. There needed to be a way to have the community aspect of a group but with the respect for personhood, living ideas, and wonderful literature of a Charlotte Mason education. We also heard from parents who wanted to use AO in a co-op or cottage school or who had a large family and wanted to combine as much as possible. So we streamlined and rearranged Years 1–8 into an abridged version of AmblesideOnline, called AO for Groups, in time for the 2017—2018 school year. We eventually hope to have AO for Groups through high school. I'm letting the other members of the Advisory rest for a bit, but I have plans to bring this up soon. . . .

## Can We Make This Method Even Clearer to Understand?

A local mom who was starting a C.M. cottage school in my area suggested weekly short readings for parents unfamiliar with Charlotte Mason to help them grasp key C.M. concepts. After all, their children have assigned reading. Why shouldn't parents also have their own assigned reading? Busy adults surrounded by cell phones, streaming videos, Facebook, and Instagram in between their own work and shuttling kids to and from activities may have a harder time focusing on a lengthy article—but they might find a couple of paragraphs every week manageable.

That was a fascinating idea: simply and concisely, yet comprehensively and accurately, explaining the C.M. method in 36 brief snippets. In fact, I stayed up until 3:00 a.m. and had almost the entire body of Patio Chats completed by morning. Now a parent (or C.M. teacher) can read a brief explanation (300–500 words) of some key C.M. concept each week, reflect on it or discuss it with other parents or teachers, perhaps use it as a foundation for a Charlotte Mason study group, and gain a foundational grasp of the main aspects of a C.M. education over the course of a school year.

Extra focus (three separate Chats) was given to personhood because every other principle is an acknowledgment and extension of the child's personhood. The Charlotte Mason method accepts the child as a full-fledged person—not a thing who will someday be a bona-fide citizen, but a complete person with needs, desires, and rights. The C.M. method is built around meeting the needs of this young person with dignity and respect, while teaching him that he has a responsibility to treat others with the same dignity and respect. The C.M. method revolves around seeing the child as a legitimate person. (Did I just define C.M. in a dozen words?) Once an adult can grasp this concept, she will never look at a child the same way. The rest is just details.

The remaining weeks cover the details that extend from personhood, many taken from the twenty principles that Charlotte Mason listed to define her method—details like atmosphere, narration, short lessons, language arts, and habits.

## What's Next?

The AmblesideOnline curriculum has been around for more than twenty years, and we've heard from parents (and experienced ourselves) that it has been successful at educating children for college, military, or just about any career imaginable. Charlotte Mason said, "People are naturally divided into those who read and think and those who do not read or think" (*A Philosophy of Education*, p. 31). Students educated with AO demonstrate an ability to read and think (and write!). We know it works. But we also know there's more to the picture than curriculum.

The missing component to AmblesideOnline, for some families, is community. There's a reason homeschool co-ops are so popular. People weren't designed to exist in isolation. Children need peers, and parents need support. That's why AO for Groups (AO4G) was created. My dream is to see AmblesideOnline taken beyond individual families and used in group settings—perhaps two or three families using AO4G in a one-room school type of setting, or a co-op holding classes at a church where each parent/teacher takes on one age group with additional special classes for art or organized sports, or a cottage school on a tight budget that could save costs by not having to pay for a curriculum license. (AO does have restrictions on how our curriculum can be used, but our primary concerns are that our curriculum stay on our own website and that a curriculum fee not be included in tuition.)

In our work with AmblesideOnline, we've seen changes in perceptions about Charlotte Mason methods. When we first started, we saw a need to clarify what was and wasn't part of a C.M. education. Moms often implemented a couple of C.M. things—perhaps narration, or outside walks, or even daily teatime—and considered that they were giving their children a comprehensive C.M. education. By 2017, we saw it swing in the opposite direction: moms were burning themselves out trying to do everything letter-perfect to meet some unrealistic standard. We found ourselves telling them to relax, not to stress over getting every detail perfect, and to allow some leeway to adjust to what works for individual families. Perhaps it will swing back in the other direction in the future. Who knows?

## To Sum Up

From the beginning, AmblesideOnline has always felt like God's work. In addition to staying true to Charlotte Mason's principles, a core factor uniting all the Advisory in this work has been that it was meant to be shared with families for free—at no profit to ourselves. For the first ten years, we paid for the webhost and domain out of our own pockets. Since we've started using affiliate links for books, we haven't had to pay to offer AmblesideOnline to the world; it has paid for itself.

Over the years, we have heard countless stories of families whose children became excited about reading through AO's living books or found a passion through the varied subjects that AO schedules. We are now seeing students who started using AmblesideOnline in first grade and graduated after twelve years of AO succeeding in college or careers. That's an entire generation of AO students! We've heard about families overseas and missionaries on a shoe-string budget who were able to give their children a quality of education they never could have afforded because AO offered it online free.

Our passion has always been to provide the treasures of a C.M. education to anyone—from the rural family with dial-up internet, to the parents trying to provide the best education they can from an old computer running seven-year-old software, to the mom who wants her children to be well-educated but free is all she can afford, to the family on the mission field who has limited bandwidth but must get all their resources online because there's no way they can afford to have books shipped overseas. Providing a "liberal education for all" means not forgetting these families. It means keeping the website simple, without images that have to load or features that depend on JavaScript to make things load properly. It means making sure that any time we list a hard-to-find book, we also list an option for the parent who can't afford to pay exorbitant prices for a rare out-of-print book. We have been amazed and awed to hear of families using AO in some of the most remote corners of the world and children being blessed with this kind of education in places we never dreamed of.

But it hasn't been all smooth. In 2001, there was some discussion about the direction of the project. We reconfirmed our vision of keeping it homespun, grassroots, and free. It was that situation that made a name change necessary, as well as the addition of a couple of people to replace those who moved on.

We've seen multiple online programs pop up that look very similar in format to AmblesideOnline, mostly appealing to people with specific interests within the Charlotte Mason community. We've seen our booklists turn up on other websites—in one case, with a few books swapped out and a note crediting the whole project to someone else. We've seen the C.M. Series with our own footnotes and annotations turn up for sale on Amazon. One of us even purchased a reprint of one of C.M.'s books, only to discover our own annotations and realize that she had just paid money to buy something that was downloaded straight from our own website! Various publishers have asked to publish all or part of our website for their profit. Some people have attempted to persuade moms that AO can only be done well with a "real" teacher in order to market their online classes through our e-groups. Others spent years telling people we were doing C.M. wrong while promoting their own C.M. project. Between 2009 and 2011, I put a couple of years of volunteer work into a curriculum project that I was told would bring Charlotte Mason to desperate children through charter schools, only to find out later that it was always intended to be marketed to C.M. homeschoolers, including those within the AO community.

These things have been discouraging, sometimes heartbreaking, and even made me occasionally wonder whether it was worth it. Yet I knew this was a worthwhile work we were doing; the imitation and competition only confirmed that what we had to offer was of value. The times I was most discouraged, Galatians 6:9 came to mind: "Let us not become weary in doing good" (NIV). So I felt like this was not our work but God's, and I needed to continue in spite of the struggles.

As our own Advisory children have graduated, we have not stopped working to support and encourage Charlotte Mason moms. Our Advisory members have been busy publishing books, giving seminars, and editing or improving the website. Our Auxiliary members have also been busy with podcasts, homeschool events, and Charlotte Mason projects. Some of the moms who started with us back in 1999 have graduated their own children by now but are taking Charlotte Mason's ideas into their communities in the form of schools, cottage schools, tutorials, and adult education. The proliferation of retired C.M. homeschool moms in local communities is a force in education unlike anything we've seen before, and we are excited about the potential for that to make a difference in a climate of increased interest in the liberal arts.

Our vision has always been moms in the trenches helping other moms in their efforts to implement a C.M. education, and we love to see our AO moms pay it forward by creating something of use to other homeschool moms and offering it in the same spirit in which we've offered AmblesideOnline—freely, out of a desire to bless another mom. All of those little offerings amount to an entire network of helps for a mom struggling to homeschool her children. New moms who lack the confidence to trust their instincts are so often the target of every product and service that seeks to part a homeschool mom and her money! Our greatest wish is that AmblesideOnline would be liberating to that new mom—a way for her to start educating her children right away while freeing her up to read and learn about all the benefits of this way of education as she goes.

We continue to pray for AO moms and the direction to take this ministry. Our own children are beginning to homeschool a whole new generation of children, and their primary concerns aren't the concerns we had when we first started homeschooling. The world isn't the same. We worried about whether homeschooling was legal and whether our children would be properly socialized. Today's children are surrounded by video games, cell phones, iPads, and social media that have to be navigated and often compete for children's attention. Some of our own graduates have used AO with foster children who have their own issues to work through, and that isn't a situation we had on our radar when we put AO together. We're excited to see what's next in AmblesideOnline's future as this way of educating brings joy and freedom to a whole new generation of children.

# Wendi: 'The Parents' Review' and How It Came to You

In 1890, in conjunction with establishing the Parents' Union, Miss Mason also began publishing and editing a monthly periodical for supporting the families and schools using her methods. It was called *The Parents' Review* (PR). The journal was sent to parents and teachers of Charlotte Mason's schools and to families who used her correspondence programs for homes. Miss Mason edited it until her death in 1923. That was roughly a thousand pages a year for thirty years, in addition to her other work.

At the end of each year, in common with most periodicals of the time, bound copies of that year's magazines were compiled into a single volume. You can read more about it and see a picture of one of those bound volumes on the AO website. You can also read a variety of articles representing many years' worth of back issues on our website.

Where did they all come from? Some were given to us by diligent scholars who had gone to libraries and made photocopies of articles. But the majority of them come from volumes the Advisory owns. How did we acquire them? I think it's a fascinating story, and one that illustrates the near-miraculous teamwork that goes on behind the scenes at AO.

Several years ago, Advisory member Anne was browsing used books online and discovered a set of nine bound PR volumes being sold in Ireland. She shared the link with the rest of us, mainly as a curiosity. "Isn't that interesting?" we thought. "Wouldn't that be lovely?" we mused, a little wistfully. And then, "Why couldn't we?" suggested somebody. I don't remember for certain which of us made that leap, but I think it might have been Karen. We talked about that a bit, and then "Why couldn't we?" changed to "Why shouldn't we?", and shortly it became "Well, of course, we must!" Soon we were excitedly discussing ways and means to accomplish what had just the day before seemed unimaginable.

The Advisory agreed that we would pool our funds, each of us contributing what we could. Because we didn't want to risk another second of time, I purchased them, trusting my fellow Advisory members to get their shares to me in time to pay the bill. After several confusing attempts to get my bank to clear a debit charge from Ireland, the volumes were then shipped to my house.

For about a week, I was the proud possessor of more PR volumes than any other known person in America owned or possibly had seen all at one time. It was a heady feeling. During the days I had those volumes in my own hot little hands, I may or may not have been seen to stroke them madly and hiss "my preciousssss" over them. I will neither confirm nor deny. (Big Grin)

After emailing the other Advisory members multiple times to taunt them a little, gloat a bit, and share excerpts from the volumes I was greedily skimming through, I finally managed to repackage the volumes separately, drive to town, and mail each of the other Advisory their own copies. (Lynn Bruce and I each bought two of the volumes, and that left one each for the remaining members).

One of the two I chose was volume II. I chose this one in particular because I'd previously visited the Library of Congress looking specifically for volume II and learned that somebody had stolen the LOC copy. I had wanted the article on teaching chronology and creating a Book of Centuries. I chose my second volume merely because it was not one of the oldest and was not in the best condition of the remaining volumes. I didn't want to be too greedy since I had my volume II.

We spent a few lovely weeks skimming our respective volumes and sharing gems we found with each other on our email list. Then we began the process of getting the articles online. I typed a few by hand. So did one or two of my daughters. Leslie collected volunteers to do the others. Some of the Advisory mailed their volumes to Leslie for photographing. Leslie would share photographed pages with volunteers, who would type from the images so Leslie could mail back the volumes to their anxious owners.

I think my other volume (I don't even remember for sure which one it is) was largely already on our website, thanks to the Library of Congress and other volunteers. But volume II was special to me. For years, Leslie asked me to mail it to her so she could photograph it, but I couldn't bear to let it leave my house, and after several bad experiences, I didn't trust our postal service. Then a near-miracle occurred. All the Advisory were on the same continent at the same time, and we were able to free up a few days at the same time. They came to my house. This was the very first time all of us were together in person—at least ten years after we'd begun working together! It was exciting and a rich blessing.

During their all-too-short stay, Leslie was able to explain what she needed to my daughter Rebecca (who was also our chief cook for the visit so that I could devote all my time to playing with my friends). After the Advisory returned home, Rebecca spent a few painstaking hours photographing all 959 pages of that precious volume II so we could finally get it to Leslie for copying. We sent it to her as a file (or several files) of images so that my volume stayed here with its doting mummy.

And that is the story of how and why our wonderful volunteers on the AO Forum are able to type up an article from volume II (along with articles from other volumes). And we owe much thanks to all our volunteers as well as to our Typing Subforum's moderator, Cathleen Waitz. For this ongoing work, articles are proofread, compared with the originals, and finally Leslie puts them on the website. There, volume II of the PR is at last available for free reading by anybody with access to the internet, along with articles from multiple other volumes.

All it took was Leslie's grand idea—

and all the hard work, blood, sweat, tears, laughter, and love that have gone into that grand idea,

a serendipitous online discovery,

another wild idea,

cooperation amongst the Advisory members,

cheerful and generous husbands,

pooled funds,

a debit card,

communication betwixt Ireland and a bank in Colorado,

the internet,

the post office,

various Advisory progeny,

several cameras,

further cooperation and unspoken but unanimous agreement among the Advisory that our purpose was to share rather than make a profit from the *Parents' Reviews,*

countless volunteers (I wish I could name them all) who have been tirelessly typing,

a forum and a forum moderator who helps keep the project on track,

proofreaders,

and an always generous outpouring of God's grace over the AO endeavor.

*(2013 post from the Advisory's blog,* Archipelago*)*

Note: Additional articles continue to be posted as often as they can be typed and proofread.

## Karen: Once upon a Time

Once upon a time, I thought I was going to homeschool using a well-known boxed curriculum. There is no need to explain the reasons behind this assumption. That was simply the situation. Fortunately for my children, they were too young for school at that stage of their lives, and before my eldest turned six, I had been introduced to Charlotte Mason.

When I first read *For the Children's Sake* by Susan Schaffer Macaulay in 1994, I found that she quoted someone named Charlotte Mason over and over again. I had never heard of her. Because I like to read original sources, it was my natural inclination to see for myself where all the quotes had come from, so I ordered Charlotte Mason's six-volume set of educational writings. I started on volume 1, *Home Education*, right away, but it would be years before I completed all six. I have that very same set still. It's much the worse for wear, but I'm reluctant to begin reading from a different set because these pink books are comfortable old friends. They have been with me nearly thirty years—my window into the mind of one of the finest thinkers I have ever known.

As I read through Charlotte Mason's volumes, I discovered that she, too, quotes and mentions a whole host of other writers, some of whom I knew and many others that I did not. By the time I had gotten through all six volumes, I was truly enamored by the thoroughness and completeness of her educational ideas. I was in awe of how prolific a writer she was, but I also had an inkling of just how prolific a reader she was.

Because I wanted to understand Charlotte Mason more deeply, I embarked on what has become a lifelong project that I will never complete: "What did Charlotte Mason read?" I wanted to read it too. I did not know that shadowing her reading journey would put me in touch with the deep philosophical thinking of the world through many centuries, but so it was.

I began with Sir Walter Scott's Waverly novels. I don't love them as much as Charlotte Mason did, so I've read only a few. Wordsworth and Milton were easy. I was an English major in college, and I'd had a whole class on the English Romantic poets (Wordsworth was the most prominent among them) and another on Milton. I still owned my college texts with my sophomore and junior years' marginalia, so I had another look at them, marveling at the educational insights Charlotte Mason took from the poets as she had from the novelists.

But I didn't want to read only the literature she read; I wanted to read the educational books and the philosophers' writings that she had read as well. I wasn't living in the United States at the time, but it was the dawn of the text-based internet, and Project Gutenberg and a few other sites made Milton and Erasmus and Plutarch available to me. I was able to track down Comenius's *Great Didactic* (the source of the phrase "a liberal education for all") and part of Quintilian's *Institutio Oratoria* (although I suspect that Charlotte Mason read about Quintilian, not Quintilian himself).*

As I read the writings of well-known educators throughout history, I picked out the best bits and made them the taglines that I attached to my email signature. Here are a few examples:

> "We know numbers who, without acquaintance with rhetorical rules, are more eloquent than many who have learnt these; but we know no one who is eloquent without having read and listened to the speeches and

---

* Charlotte Mason may have encountered Quintilian in *An Introduction to the History of Educational Theories* by Oscar Browning. She included this book as part of the reading in her Mothers' Education Course. Also of interest is the fact that Oscar Browning was around when the PNEU was formed, and he contributed several articles to the *Parents' Review* in its first year of publication.

debates of eloquent men. For even the art of grammar, which teaches correctness of speech, need not be learnt by boys, if they have the advantage of growing up and living among men who speak correctly." (Augustine, *On Christian Doctrine*)

"Grammar being but an introduction to the understanding of authors, if it be made too long or exquisite to the learner, it in a manner mortifieth his courage: And by that time he cometh to the most sweet and pleasant reading of old authors, the spark of fervent desire of learning is extinct with the burden of grammar, like as a little fire is soon quenched with a great heap of small sticks: so that it can never come to the principal logs where it should long burn in a great pleasant fire." (Sir Thomas Elyot, *Boke Named the Governour*, spelling modernized)

## You've Got Mail

I was profoundly blessed to connect with women who were as interested in all these obscure ideas as I was. It's not much fun to dig a gem out of a dusty old volume or find a treasure among pages of archaic prose and then have no one to share it with. I shared everything I was learning with the larger Charlotte Mason community year after year, and they repaid my hours of reading and research tenfold and thirtyfold and a hundredfold by being genuinely interested in the things I discovered.

Others have already spoken of the connections and close friendships we formed in our email communications. We shared the books we were reading ourselves, the books we were reading with our children, and our attempts to follow Charlotte Mason's methods at every level of learning. Without realizing it, we were partaking of a long tradition. The frequency of postal deliveries crops up often in older books. Heroes and heroines sent and received letters with great regularity. Jane Austen gave us some of the best glimpses. In *Pride and Prejudice*, Elizabeth Bennet is delighted to finally receive a letter from her sister Jane, little suspecting it will bring her dreadful news, which was also first conveyed in an express letter that couldn't wait for the regular post. Colonel Brandon, likewise, had to disappoint his friends in *Sense and Sensibility* because an express letter arrived with an urgent message.

Even the regular post was delivered often. In Victorian London, mail routes were run every hour, twelve times per day! In less populated areas, it was usually delivered twice each day. You might send a note in the morning post and expect to receive a reply the same day or certainly by the next morning. People kept a bountiful supply of paper, ink, and pens. Mail received in the morning might require an immediate reply, and ladies and gentlemen alike would sit down for an hour or so after breakfast to write their letters. Letter writing was a very important part of socializing and communicating before the advent of the telephone, and it had a revival with the advent of email.

Such frequent communication in writing had virtually disappeared by the end of the twentieth century, but suddenly here we were, doing exactly the same thing again. "You've got mail!" the computer told us triumphantly—not twice a day but many, many times a day. Reading mail and replying right away became, again, a daily part of our lives. But this time it was all electronic. Our mail was sent with the push of a button and arrived to our friends located far, far away in almost the same moment.

Many of us have saved older emails just as folks once saved bundles of handwritten letters and even drafts of their own letters that they sent. While fossicking through some old files, I found this from an email I wrote dated April 1, 2001: "I would dearly love to write a book on 'Charlotte Mason and the Classical Tradition of Education,' but I'm not sure who would read it."

My oldest child was eleven at the time, but my reading from the books Charlotte Mason had read had awakened this interest. In

2014, that wish because a reality with the publication of my book *Consider This*, which carries that exact subtitle—*Charlotte Mason and the Classical Tradition.* In 2001 I didn't know who would read a book like that, but in 2023 I know that there were many interested readers after all.

## Magnanimity

In 2002, I launched an e-zine—an electronic magazine. I wanted it to be a place where we could keep on learning and sharing in the spirit of Charlotte Mason and the PNEU. In the first issue, I wrote the following:

> I'm pleased to offer you the first issue of *Magnanimity.* The purpose of this newsletter is not to encourage or uplift you, not to share useful internet links or homeschool tips, and not to entertain you with anecdotes or supply you with information about homeschooling in general. I hope we may do all those things from time to time, but the purpose of this newsletter is to supply us with nourishment for the mind.
>
> Charlotte Mason offers us an analogy, which has been used by many fine educators, including those of classical antiquity. She compares the action of the mind upon knowledge to the action of the digestive system upon food.
>
> Just as we can eat food that is tasty but empty of nutrition, so we can fill our minds with tidbits of tantalizing knowledge, making us feel full but failing to nourish our heart and spirit. The only proper "mind food," according to Charlotte Mason, is living ideas. These ideas are best appropriated by means of living books, though ideas come to us through other means as well.

> With this analogy in hand, the purpose of this newsletter is to offer substantial mind food that will give you something to think about, to stretch your understanding, and to better equip you for the challenging task of educating your sons and daughters.

Didn't I have grand ideas for that newsletter? Look what I wanted to do! My 2002 self, whose oldest child hadn't turned twelve yet, wanted to draw everyone's attention to the great ideas that were so inspiring to me.

I explained how the meaning of the title suited the intent of the effort:

> *Magnanimity* implies that education is not only about the mind or intellect but about broadening and strengthening the character, enlarging the heart and soul, as well as the mind, of man. This "greatness of spirit" recalls to mind John 10:10, where Jesus said, "I am come that they might have life, and that they might have it more abundantly."
>
> Man is not only a physical creation but has a spiritual, nonmaterial side as well. There is more to life than physical well-being, and *magnanimity* is a reminder of the side that we most want to grow and mature. Those of us who are educating our own children are seeking the means of bringing magnanimity into their lives. In the process, we desire it and seek it for ourselves.
>
> Here a little and there little, line upon line, and precept upon precept, we learn and grow and stretch ourselves. Charlotte Mason tells us that the mind is spiritual (meaning nonmaterial), and education worthy of the name seeks to develop this spiritual mind as well as inform the intellect. This newsletter can be no more than one small

impulse, but mind and spirit are hungry, and I hope that what is contained here will serve as a stepping-stone to wider reading and spirit-growth for each reader—not only in a religious sense, but growth of that nonmaterial mind with which God has endowed us.

Magnanimity—greatness or fullness of life—begins with a love of virtue and a desire to attain it. Milton says of his pupils that he wanted to "win them early to the love of virtue." It does not happen all at once, but high ideals must be considered. It is too easy to lose sight of the higher goals if we keep our sights set only on the rough ground at our feet.

Alfred North Whitehead, noted philosopher and educator, reminds us that "at the dawn of our European civilization, men started with the full ideals which should inspire education, and...gradually our ideals have sunk to square with our practice." Rather than thinking about the hearts and character of our children, we look myopically at the number of books read, the workbooks finished, the diplomas collected.

Lift your eyes for a moment from the curriculum guide, teacher's manual, math problems, and state-imposed guidelines. Look at the high goal of education: a virtuous man or woman who loves the Lord—an individual who thinks rightly and acts righteously. This is not the work of a day or a week or a year. Progress is not measured by checking off a finished assignment. Though we must give attention to the details of the journey, fix your eyes on the goal as often as possible, though you can do no more than take one step at a time.

> Even when you know you have far to go and have not attained, the sight of your goal is there to inspire you and encourage you. The journey itself is the important thing. Anyone can stand far off and look at a mountain, but only those willing to make the climb will achieve the height. The journey itself will increase your ability to go on. If the peak is never reached, we may still climb higher than we would have done if we had never begun at all!
>
> Physical muscles atrophy when they go unused, and so do spiritual and mental ones. If you are making that journey to grow and strengthen your heart and mind, a book that seems too hard today may not be hard at all next year or in five years. *Magnanimity* is a grand-sounding word, but it is a grand education that we want. We will not be satisfied but ever hungry for more knowledge, more strength of spirit, more greatness of mind.

As I write this now, my 2023 self marvels at the seeds of ideas that were there in 2002. More than twenty years ago, I was hoping to inspire a love of virtue and bravely lifting my eyes to a peak I was never sure I'd be able to reach. And indeed I have not. I'm climbing still, but I no longer imagine that there is a final goal—a pinnacle that, if I reach it, will represent the absolute achievement of all that I hoped to do. Twenty years later, I know that the journey was the point all along and that the path by no means raised me up higher and higher with every step but wound through valleys and byways that obscured any potential final goal at times. I catch a glimpse of a peak now and then, but I do not imagine I am always scaling toward higher heights. The journey has been what mattered most, and the fellowship of my companions along the way a constant blessing. The peaks and pinnacles are out there, and they are still inspiring, but I am happy to read books that interest me without worrying about achieving any goals.

## Great Ideas Endure

I didn't keep up writing that newsletter very long—just a little over a year. I really enjoyed writing the articles—the first time I'd ever done anything quite like that—but the schedule and deadline were hard to maintain while I was busy homeschooling three children (and there would soon be a fourth!) and working on AmblesideOnline. Most of my writing for many, many years continued to be in the form of emails, although I tried my hand at blogging for a while when blogging was first in vogue. Whatever the avenue of communication, my desire to share about all the things I was reading and learning in order to contribute a little to the intellectual and spiritual well-being of my fellow homeschool mothers never went away.

Eventually, it would take the form of writing actual books—a dream from my childhood. I even wrestled a few of those fat pink volumes of Charlotte Mason's into a form more accessible for contemporary readers.

I continue to read what Charlotte Mason wrote (and I think everyone should), and I still want to read the things that Charlotte Mason read. I will never catch up. In spite of the mountain of actual books in my to-be-read stack and the list of titles I still plan to purchase, I keep going back and rereading those pink volumes. Having reread them many times (I lost count a long time ago), I have discovered something: every time that I go back and read a volume, I learn something new. Charlotte Mason brought so much wisdom and deep understanding to the topic of education that it is impossible to appropriate all she had to say in a single reading, or even two or three. As I read the writing of other educators throughout history and return to Charlotte Mason, I find that she has trod the same ground, considered the same questions, uncovered the same vital principles. And beyond all that, she had the ability to develop sound practices based upon the principles—practices that make the principles living and effective rather than abstract and academic.

And it has always been that way! This year I've been reading *School Education*. As always, I've gleaned a few new insights, but this is what I wrote in an email dated December 31, 2001, when I was leading a book study through this same volume. We were on chapter 15:

> The more I read Charlotte Mason, the more I appreciate her! *(2023 note: Some things never change!)* We are moving here from the philosophical part of the book into the more practical. You've all been very patient with the philosophy part, but if you've been champing at the bit to get to something practical, we are finally there.
>
> "School Books and Education"—Charlotte Mason opens with a lengthy anecdote about some schoolgirls (teenagers, actually) who were very inspired by their history lessons. She uses this story to show us a moral: What kind of books delight and impassion students?
>
> There is an often-quoted bit here that's worth repeating: "We need not ask what the girl or boy likes. *She* very often likes the twaddle of goody-goody story books, *he* likes condiments, highly-spiced tales of adventure. We are all capable of liking mental food of a poor quality and a titillating nature; and possibly such food is good for us when our minds are in need of an elbow-chair; but our spiritual life is sustained on other stuff, whether we be boys or girls, men or women" (p. 168).
>
> With reluctant readers, we sometimes try to coax them into reading by way of this type of literature, but again,

while there may be a time for it ("When our minds are in need of elbow chair"), second-rate literature will not feed the mind and spirit of anyone.

Charlotte Mason has some hard words for the textbooks of her day. More valuable for us, probably, are the hints she gives about what kinds of books we *should* be using: "Living ideas can be derived only from living minds" (p. 169). This living spark, she says, only comes via a teacher if the teacher has given original thought to a subject. Otherwise, our best teachers are the authors of the best books.

As a side note, I think there is some valuable information in this chapter about the role of the teacher in a C.M.-style education. "What he [the pupil] wants of his teacher is moral and mental discipline, sympathy, and direction" (p. 179). This is not the hands-off method of John Holt or an unschooler. The teacher is imposing discipline—mental and moral. The teacher is supplying direction, not leaving it to the students. And, very importantly, the teacher is a sympathetic learner and listener, who shares both in the labor and in the delight of the learning process.

The quote "Thou hast set my feet in a large room" is from Psalm 31:8. I've always found these words thrilling: "The question is not,—how much does the youth *know*? when he has finished his education—but how much does he *care*" (p. 170)? Our job is not to fill up our children with facts and information but to assist them in forming relationships with every area of knowledge available to mankind. As Charlotte Mason says of our children,

"We owe it to them to initiate an immense number of interests" (p. 170).

When we think of education in this way, it actually becomes much less threatening, I think. We don't have to worry about covering this or that material. We have simply to open the doors—via great books, art, and music—and let our children make the relationships themselves. We cannot make them care about anything, but we can provide them the most interesting and enticing way of learning about a subject. We should never, never, never kill a child's delight and interest in a subject with too much lecturing, questioning, or school paraphernalia.

Elsewhere in the series (volume 5, *Formation of Character*), she discusses the way in which Shakespeare is sometimes taught—with lots of analysis. This ruins the pure enjoyment of the characters and the play. I'm reading another book right now, and the author (Alfred North Whitehead) says the same thing—he says such teachers should be arrested for soul-murder.

The next chapter will have few more specific ideas about schoolbooks, but the big message in this chapter is to choose them carefully, taking care that they are not dry and dull compendiums of facts but full of living, vitalizing (life-giving) ideas. If you are aware of the specific suggestions Charlotte Mason gives for children, you know that she has tremendous respect for the power of their minds.

As she says at the beginning of this chapter, there is nothing really new here. We've heard this before, and the use of living books and respect for the child are the hallmarks of Charlotte Mason's educational philosophy. This chapter just reiterates for us the importance of these principles. "The great work of education is to inspire children with vitalising ideas as to every relation of life, every department of knowledge, every subject of thought; and to give deliberate care to the formation of those habits of the good life which are the outcome of vitalising ideas. In this great work we seek and assuredly find the co-operation of the Divine Spirit, whom we recognise, in a sense rather new to modern thought, as the supreme Educator of mankind in things that have been called secular, fully as much as in those that have been called sacred" (p. 173).

Have you experienced the kind of *vitalizing* books Charlotte Mason is talking about? I think that experience is absolutely necessary for the parent/teacher using her methods. You really need to know what a living book does for your mind in order to guide your students on this path. Would you care to share a book or two that has truly enlightened you this way? One of my email signature quotes is paraphrased from an observation by Oliver Wendell Holmes: "A mind, once stretched by a new idea, never regains its original dimensions." What book has done this for you?

Also, do you have any thoughts about the role of the teacher in a Charlotte Mason education? I think this is an area that is misunderstood sometimes. This chapter is one of two places in the series (that I can recall) where the role is somewhat defined in a positive way. (That is, she tells us what we should be doing, not what we shouldn't be doing.) Do you think the role of direction

> and discipline is better than the "traditional teacher" model or child-led method of instruction?
>
> Have you seen some school subject light a fire in your children like the girls in the story? Not every child will love the same things, but what has really taken root in their minds? Share an anecdote or two from this past year.
>
> I know it's a new year, and we're all staying up late, but let's resolve to discuss some great ideas in 2002!

Reading what I wrote over twenty years ago, I am somewhat startled to find that my enthusiasm and appreciation have not waned. The things I was saying then I find myself saying now, but they do not feel dull and repetitious to me. I still want to talk about great ideas in 2023. As always, I resort to the analogy of the mind as a living organism needing ideas for true nourishment. Ideas do not grow stale. They are living seeds, and going back to them again and again brings opportunity for new insight and refreshment of soul.

## The Waves Prevail

I have always enjoyed this word picture of feeding the mind. So many parallels can be drawn between our mind-meals and the meals we feed our physical bodies. It doesn't matter how many pizzas you've eaten in your life, or how many grilled steaks, or how many homemade tacos. When you are hungry and you are offered a plate with a much-loved meal, you will partake with great enjoyment and be filled and nourished. Old favorites are still delicious.

So while I keep reading books that Charlotte Mason read—Coleridge's *Treatise on Method* or Fouillée's *Education from a National Standpoint*—I come back to her volumes again and again.

I find her able to teach me something new, or if not new, it's just as satisfying and soul-filling to hear the same truths over again.

In an odd juxtaposition of events, I found myself reading that same chapter from *School Education* again while I was working on this project. Within that chapter, I found Charlotte Mason a little worried that she was repeating herself too, but she didn't mind.

> I daresay the reader will find that I have said before what I shall say now. But we are not like those men of Athens who met to hear and to tell some new thing; and he will, I know, bear with me because he will recognise how necessary it is to repeat again and again counsels which are like waves beating against the rock of an accepted system of things. But, in time, the waves prevail and the rock wears away; so we go to work with good hope. (p. 164)

The world at large has a view of education that is like that rock. It seems insurmountable, fixed, and unmoving. But we keep sharing the ideas of Charlotte Mason, the vision of a better way, year after year. New families decide to homeschool. New children turn six every year and begin at the beginning of *Our Island Story* and *Paddle-to-the-Sea*. Educators discover Charlotte Mason for the first time and begin reading her volumes just as we did. Sometimes they are schoolteachers who want to learn how to use Charlotte Mason's living principles in their classrooms. The waves are wearing away the rock after all.

So I don't mind that I'm still saying today what I have said before. Thomas Rooper—an educator, an author, and a colleague of Charlotte Mason—dedicated his book *Educational Studies and Addresses* to her. Addressing the PNEU, he wrote, "Sound principles that are old may easily be laid on the shelf and forgotten, unless in each successive generation a few industrious people can be found who will take the trouble to draw them forth from the storehouse" (p. 7).

Charlotte Mason was an intelligent and courageous educator who did just that—laid hold of vital educational principles and brought them out as clearly as she could for her generation. We hope we have had a small part in the same work, bringing the principles to families in the form of programs that can be used freely by anyone, anywhere who has access to the internet. It has been said that the sun never sets on AmblesideOnline because it is being used by families all around the globe. Charlotte Mason's legacy is living and growing, and we are thrilled to know that we have been fellow laborers in that great work, side by side with every homeschool mom who reads a chapter, closes the book, and says, "It's time to narrate what we read."

Charlotte Mason assures us, "In this field small efforts are honoured with great rewards, and we perceive that the education we are giving exceeds all that we intended or imagined" (*School Education*, p. 163). I hope that you will find this to be true and that we keep the waves of enthusiasm in motion, wearing away the rocks.

## Anne: How I Got My Charlotte Mason Books

For the first few years of our family's homeschooling, I borrowed Charlotte Mason's volumes—one or two or three at a time—from a Christian homeschool group's lending library. But at some point I started wishing that I had my own.

There's a secondhand bookstore downtown, the sort that buys and trades as well as sells. My husband had been digging out a few old books that he thought might be worth something, including an extra Bible from his childhood. We drove down to the bookstore, and while he negotiated with the store owner, I browsed. And there they were: all six pink and white volumes. The set wasn't cheap, at least for our budget—it was priced at something like thirty or forty dollars. Of course I wanted it, but I didn't think we were going to be able to afford it just then.

This is what happened: most of my husband's books were worth only a few dollars, even in store credit. But that particular Bible turned out to be a very desirable one, and they gave him an unheard-of thirty or forty dollars in credit.

When I showed him the pink volumes, he said, "That's what we'll do with it then."

And the rest is dog-eared, margin-noted, Advisory-autographed history.

(*Email, 2023*)

## Snippet 1

*One day in 2017, we were discussing who would send the announcement for a particular project while life went on in the background.*

**Donna-Jean:**

Are we all in agreement that we are good with this so far?

**Karen:**

I think we should [announce this], yes.

**Leslie:**

I wrote up a little promotional paragraph. I think it could be posted, and I could do it as soon as I get home from basketball camp—in a couple hours. Yes?

**Anne:**

Okay here. (Now doing the next weird thing: trying to slim down a thrift-store skirt.)

**Leslie:**

I can match weirdness for weirdness. I carry tiny scissors in my purse, so I was sitting on the floor cutting up note paper at basketball. I do enjoy paper.

**Wendi:**

Definitely you, Leslie. You should announce it.

Just Fix the Plate

Children no more come into the world without provision for dealing with knowledge than without provision for dealing with food. They bring with them not only that intellectual appetite, the desire of knowledge, but also an enormous, an unlimited power of attention to which the power of retention (memory) seems to be attached, as one digestive process succeeds another, until the final assimilation. "Yes," it will be said, "they are capable of much curiosity and consequent attention but they can only occasionally be beguiled into attending to their lessons." Is not that the fault of the lessons, and must not these be regulated as carefully with regard to the behaviour of mind as the children's meals are with regard to physical considerations? (*A Philosophy of Education*, pp. 14–15)

## Karen: A Charlotte Mason Teacher

Homeschool moms coming to Charlotte Mason can feel overwhelmed by the inclusion of so many different things. In addition to teaching basic subjects, they are overwhelmed at the idea of teaching art appreciation and watercolor and nature lore, as well as Shakespeare, poetry, and music. How can a homeschool mom do all of that while keeping up with the baby, the laundry, and the meals? There is a philosophical problem here. Addressing it will probably ease the burden and make a Charlotte Mason education feel much more attainable. The problem (I think) is the word *teach*. That implies a certain picture, in which you, the teacher, are imparting knowledge to your student while he is receiving it from you. That's not the relationship between teacher and pupil in a Charlotte Mason paradigm.

Let me recast the question in a different context. Suppose you were feeling conflicted in a different area, like this: "You mean that in addition to providing seasonally appropriate clothing, shoes, and outerwear for my schoolchild 365 days of the year and maintaining a safe shelter adequate to protect him and keep him warm, I also have to ensure that he grows taller and heavier? That his hands and feet grow, and his bones? That his blood supply increases as he grows to meet his larger size? That his heart and lungs develop greater strength to support his larger body? How am I supposed to do all that for him and look after the baby and the laundry as well?"

Do you see the problem? You aren't responsible for ensuring that your child grows larger, let alone looking after specific details like making sure his blood supply increases. He will do those things for himself—all of them, under the right conditions—and the requirement is that you provide him adequate and nourishing meals. And yes, several times per day, 365 days per year. If you think of it all at once, it's overwhelming. But you do it one day at time and one meal at a time. You consider what kind of food will make the most nutritious meals, and you even take your child's taste into account, but you'll also make it a point to introduce him to a wide variety of things and give him a chance to learn to like all the best kinds of food. And it's a big job—it takes time and money—but it's done in small increments, and one off day in appetite or indulging in extra junk food doesn't ruin the long-term effect. Your child is fed and grows physically, as he is designed to do.

That is the right picture for a Charlotte Mason paradigm. You aren't going to "teach" your child all those things any more than you are going to eat and digest your child's meals. You are just going to put that food in front of him, and he does all the rest himself. You might insist that he eat, but hunger is on your side. You are going to spread a wide feast for your child—an intellectual banquet—and make him sit down to the table. His natural appetite for knowledge works in your favor, but you don't force-feed him. He'll take what he needs intellectually, and he'll grow—oh, how he'll grow. Long before he is old enough to leave home, you will come face to face with a situation in which your child knows more than you do about something and wonder how that happened. That's how this works. You feed them; they do the growing themselves.

In that context, a Charlotte Mason education becomes no more complex than some basic meal planning. You aren't making your child's liver function properly—you're just making him a sandwich. You aren't teaching art appreciation; you're just looking a painting. Or a tree. Or reading an interesting bit of history or singing a song or enjoying a great story.

"Education is the science of relations" is the principle that lies underneath what we do and ties everything together. When you break it down into all its component parts—as you must do when you put it on paper with labels like "history" and "science" and "art"—it can feel a bit overwhelming, just as it would if you had to break down all the necessary vitamins, minerals, phytonutrients, etc., that your child needs to grow properly. But what it still looks like on a day-to-day basis is breakfast, lunch, dinner, and healthy snacks (most of the time). When we talk about the theory and philosophy of what we do—nutritional science or educational philosophy—it sounds more complicated than it actually is.

You can overcomplicate anything. Suppose you approached the making of a single meal with the same analytical micro-focus. You have to make sure that you have twenty separate ingredients, as well as bowls, pans, knives, and other utensils. You have to wash and chop carrots *and* onions *and* celery. You have to peel eight potatoes and cut them into pieces. You have to measure five different seasonings, keep the heat at the correct temperature, etc., etc., etc., and that's just the soup course. In practice, it's far less complex than it sounds on paper, and that's true for education too. When we talk about it and look at all the different bits individually, it feels like a huge, overwhelming job; but when you get in there and start doing it, things fall into place. You feel how forgiving the process can be. You have two carrots instead of four? It will be okay. Throw in some extra celery or onions or half of a chopped bell pepper. Some things are less flexible: don't mess with the baking powder measurement if you're making a cake. Experience will quickly teach you which things are flexible and which things need to be firmly adhered to.

This is firmly embedded in Charlotte Mason's principles. The twelfth principle is "Education is the science of relations." That's a little bit like "Hungry growing children need to be fed meals." You absolutely can do this if you keep "education is the science of relations" firmly in mind and don't let yourself get bogged down or overwhelmed by the details.

> "Education is the Science of Relations"; that is, that a child has natural relations with a vast number of things and thoughts: so we must train him upon physical exercises, nature, handicrafts, science and art, and upon *many living books*; for we know that our business is, not to teach him all about anything, but to help him make valid, as many as may be of [what Wordsworth called] "Those first born affinities, / That fit our new existence to existing things." (*A Philosophy of Education*, p. xxx)

Did you catch that? Our business is *not* to teach him *all* about *anything*. That's a principle (or part of one). Just fix the plate and set it in front of him. Encourage him to take a bite. Take a bite yourself and let your children know it's delicious. Listen to music. Read a book. Talk to each other about it. Observe the ants on the sidewalk. Take delight in a sunset. You don't really remind yourself every day that your children are hungry and need to be fed—that becomes a part of your life, and you live it. If you can embed "education is the science of relations" that deeply and intuitively into your educational life, you will be a Charlotte Mason teacher.

*(2018 post from* Archipelago*)*

## Lynn: On Leisure, Learning, and Large Rooms

Little did I know when I turned a page and came upon this passage well over a decade ago that my children's lives would be immeasurably changed by it:

> Our aim in Education is to give a Full Life.—We begin to see what we want. Children make large demands upon us. We owe it to them to initiate an immense number of interests. "Thou hast set my feet in a large room," should be the glad cry of every intelligent soul. Life should be all living, and not merely a tedious passing of time; not all doing or all feeling or all thinking—the strain would be too great—but, all living; that is to say, we should be in touch wherever we go, whatever we hear, whatever we see, with some manner of vital interest. We cannot give the children these interests; we prefer that they should never say they have learned botany or conchology, geology or astronomy. *The question is not,—how much does the youth know? when he has finished his education—but how much does he care? and about how many orders of things does he care? In fact, how large is the room in which he finds his feet set? and, therefore, how full is the life he has before him?*" (Charlotte Mason, *School Education*, pp. 170–171; italics mine)

Mason's writings are humbling to me because of the way Scripture flows so naturally and organically into her ideas and phrasings. In the quote above, she pays homage to Psalm 31, and in so doing she loads it with a layer of meaning that we'll miss if we're in too big a hurry (or if we never read the KJV!).

> I will rejoice and be glad in Thy mercy: for Thou hast considered my trouble; Thou hast known my soul in adversities; and hast not shut me up into the hand of the enemy: Thou hast set my feet in a large room.

David exults here in a God of magnanimity—a God who not only delivers him out of the darkness of adversity but goes far beyond mere rescue to establish David in a space of remarkable expanse and liberality. God gave David exactly what he needed, and then far more.

Mason, then, by alluding to this Psalm, is drawing upon David's exultation in God's abundant nature to assist her in giving Him glory for what that large room represents in the context of her own life: education. This is fitting because education is also a deliverance. And this deliverance, like David's, is not limited to merely being rescued from the grip of darkness, because with all that God has provided for us to learn and know, education can and should be a transcendent deliverance into a large room—a magnanimously appointed life of the mind.

In an earlier post, I echoed a borrowed thought that education is a form of repentance. We all view education as a necessity, but do we apprehend that it was necessitated by the Fall? Before sin entered into the world, man strolled in the garden with the Fount of all wisdom and knowledge. The curse that demotes us from our created state of ease to a life of toiling for our food and livelihood, fighting diseases, and suffering pain and heartache is the same curse that distanced us from wisdom and that causes us to suffer from ignorance, nonsense, and foolishness. Education is to ignorance what aspirin is to pain—both are equally weapons of our warfare against the effects of the Fall.

By asking "How large is the room in which he finds his feet set?" as a means of measuring the viability of an education, Mason is clearly drawing God into the matter, for clearly God is the one who sets our feet. And the greatest gift God gives to His people other than salvation is knowledge. When the Psalmist sang, "The Lord is my light and my salvation," he was proclaiming that both were vital to his welfare. In fact, we need knowledge from God to even know about our salvation!

Which brings me to *Leisure: The Basis of Culture*, which I am reading with Cindy Rollins' *Ordo Amoris* book group. Author Josef Pieper points out that our word for school comes from the Greek word *schola*. No surprise there. The shocker is this: *schola*, it turns out, is the Greek word for leisure.

*(What? School = leisure? On what planet? Yeah, I can almost hear you out there.)*

It is important here to clarify that leisure does not equal laziness in Pieper's context. Nor does it mean pursuing mindless, passive amusements. It means, to my mind, ceasing from anxiety and from merely utilitarian preoccupations so that one can contemplate higher things. Leisure encompasses those pursuits without which we cannot be fully human.

Why have we not acknowledged by now that the human mind, by its nature, does not learn in a state of anxiety? (Irony alert: Maybe we can't learn that because the implications make us more anxious?) We all know this from our own experience, do we not? So we should be willing to at least consider the converse—that our minds are actually wired to learn, to receive knowledge, in a state of leisure.

Here's where it gets interesting: Pieper expands on the connection between leisure (a state of nonwork) and the commandment for Sabbath rest. He muses that it is in this state of Sabbath leisure that the body of Christ convenes in worship and becomes the bodily visible bride. This state of worship-leisure, then, is incarnational in nature: the bride of Christ becomes visible not in a state of exertion and work but rather in a state of leisure. This is a beautiful thing to think about.

And it occurs to me that this state of worship-leisure also means that we bring no work, not even the spirit of work, before the Lord in His house...because He has finished the work. It is only because of this that we can come before Him in a state of Sabbath rest.

Sabbath rest means coming before the Lord in stillness, in a turning away from exertion and anxiety, so we can consecrate a space in time "to rejoice and be glad in Thy mercy." It makes sense to me, in this context, that worship is the only true source of leisure—for if we do not cast our cares upon Him, if we do not trust in His finished work, we can never be truly at rest. Worship is indeed what allows us to have leisure in our souls, for the purpose of glorifying and enjoying fellowship with God.

Which brings us full circle...

*Worship, Pieper contends, is the basis of all leisure.*

*And leisure = schola.*

*:: pause ::*

Can we concur, then, that worship is the basis for...school?

And can we then concur that school, to be based in worship, should happen in the absence of anxiety and fear, and in an atmosphere of rest and delight?

(I warn you that if you think about this very much, it might change how you go about things as early as tomorrow morning.)

Would you say your own education happened in an atmosphere defined more by leisure or by hurry, stress, and anxiety?

What would your children say about their educational atmosphere?

> *"For God hath not given us a spirit of fear, but of power, and of love, and of a sound mind" (II Timothy 1:7).*

**Addendum:** While I was battling cancer, that passage from Psalm 31 was written across my bathroom mirror in big letters for over a year, and I chanted it aloud to the Lord every day for many months. It was immensely calming—every day, without fail, these words restored me from a spirit of fear to a peaceful, sound mind. In fact, I can truly say that in these words, I found leisure for my soul in a very anxious time.

(*This post first appeared on Lynn's blog* The Beehive *in 2009. It is included here with the gracious permission of her family. Lynn added the postscript as a message of hope. During this time, her cancer was in remission.*)

## Leslie: Language Arts on the Fly

Language arts are probably the easiest part of educating with Charlotte Mason's methods. It's so deceptively simple that I've graduated three students who are proficient in language skills without ever purchasing a language arts curriculum or cracking open a spelling book. In fact, one of my graduates went on to major in English at college and was one of two subjects of a doctoral thesis on C.M.'s language arts acquisition.

What's the secret? It's this: you learn to read by reading, and you learn to write by writing. Or, to amplify it a bit, you learn to read and comprehend and know what words look like by reading, and you learn to write and spell and punctuate by using those things as you write and sometimes by noticing your own mistakes and mentally correcting them.

But what does that *look* like?

It might look like you're not doing much in the way of language arts. But there's more learning going on with C.M.'s methods than meets the eye. The details will probably look a little different from one home to the next, but here's how *we* did it.

### The Early Years

In the early preschool years, I read picture books to my kids. We did lots and lots of reading.

When they "started school" at age six or seven, they started **daily copywork**. I would write a word or two on a sheet of elementary-lined paper, and the child would copy it underneath. In some cases, the child would trace it first and then try to write it. Tracing was always more fun with a colored pencil or highlighter!

Choosing a word to write was pretty straightforward: "You liked the Peter Rabbit story we read today where he sees the white cat twitching its tail. Would you like to write 'Peter' today?" My son might say, "Can I write 'white cat' instead?" So I would write "white cat" lightly in pencil on a sheet of lined paper, and he would trace it and then copy it. Sometimes a child had definite ideas of his own about what to write. One wanted to write "Happy Birthday" every day for the two weeks before his birthday. Another wrote her own name a lot. One child went through a cowboy phase and wanted to write "horse" every day, so I let him. Usually there would be little doodles of horses or something, and those are articles of schoolwork that I still cherish (along with one son's written narrations, which were always bordered with stick figures dueling with lightsabers).

Later, when copying a single word became too easy, we moved on to short sentences, which I would write on lined paper for the child to copy underneath. It was always easy to come up with sentences—either from something going on in real life or from something we had been reading: "Balto is a good dog." "I am seven years old." "Polly is my pet horse." I usually just came up with something relevant off the top of my head. Sometimes the child already knew what he wanted to write: "I want to write, 'Molly is our new cat!'"

## Moving On

When we moved up to slightly longer sentences, I started taking things from real print. This was never difficult since we're homeschooling with real books and always surrounded with text. I would pick up a book (usually one we were using for school that day), open to what we had just read, and scan the text for a suitable sentence—something in the general vicinity of the length I wanted without any complicated spellings (no foreign names or regional dialect) or complicated punctuation. If the book would lie flat, the child could copy straight from the book. If not, I would still write it out by hand for him to copy. But since copywork at this point was still straightforward sentences, it was quick and easy for me to write it out—it took all of maybe ninety seconds.

Sometimes I put more thought and organization into it. One year I collected Bible verses from the children's Bible we were using, and we started from the shortest verse and worked our way to the longest. I picked out specific verses I wanted my children to internalize—about God's love and mercy, kindness, that sort of thing—never verses chosen to chastise the child for some besetting sin.

Later, some of my children chose their own copywork. One transcribed entire chapters from *The Lion, The Witch and the Wardrobe*. Two of my sons transcribed George Washington's *Rules of Civility*. We used a modernized copy because I wanted them copying correct spelling, not quaint antiquated English (but when my daughter did that later, she insisted on using the original). I reminded them to try to copy word by word, not letter by letter, since seeing the word as a whole is what teaches spelling. I have a collection of quotable quotes about books and reading that I collected from the internet and saved in a document, and if any of my children didn't have anything specific to write, they could use one of those.

As each child got older, the copywork increased in length but never took longer than ten minutes unless the child just liked writing.

## The Upper Years

Around the time copywork started getting to a point where I thought the child could write a sentence or two on his own, we started **written narrations**. My first child did one written narration a week (because he loved to write, took a lot of time and care on his one narration, and was doing a lot of writing on his own outside of school). With the others, I think we started with a couple a week, then once a day, and settled at two half-page narrations a day around seventh grade. Whatever wasn't written was narrated orally. In high school (around tenth grade), I started assigning **written essays.** I collected SAT-type essay questions from the internet, printed them, and cut them out. The child would draw one from the collection, and that would be his writing assignment that day.

Around the time written narrations started, we also added **studied dictation**. My general method: Open a book. Pick a sentence. Hand child the book and have him study the page or even just the paragraph containing the sentence. When he's ready, I read the sentence out loud, and he writes it. Boom—we're done.

We started dictations slow and easy: "Learn this sentence so you can write it without looking." It might be only four words long. After that seemed too easy, I made it tricky: "Learn this short paragraph with three sentences; you'll need to be able to write one of them without looking." My youngest is in the middle of this process now, and as I scan our school reading for an appropriate dictation passage, I'm starting to look for passages with quotation marks and semicolons. Today's dictation was taken from *Northanger Abbey*, the chapter we read this morning. I never choose something she can't do, and she almost never makes a mistake. If she is making mistakes, I back off and choose sentences with fewer complicated spellings, less punctuation, shorter length. The point is for her to succeed, not to catch her in a mistake. We don't do copywork on the days we do dictation; it's either one or the other. She's always happy when it's a dictation day and not a copywork day.

Does that sound too easy? It actually *is* that easy—in fact, it seems so self-evident that I feel redundant even writing it out. I find language arts to be the quickest, simplest, most painless part of a C.M. education. There's nothing to buy, no complicated curriculum to follow, no lists of vocabulary or spelling words to memorize, no contrived creative writing assignments. The whole thing takes five or ten minutes a day, and writing has never become a dreaded, tedious chore. In fact, most of my children's writing happens outside of school. With the skills they practice painlessly during school, they take off in their own time and write their own stories or plays or songs. I believe in making as little work and fuss as possible, and language arts is an area where simpler is truly better.

(*2017 post from* Archipelago)

## Wendi: The Modern Place for Old Books

Why do we use old books? We live in the twenty-first century, after all!

In general, well-written older books include richer vocabulary, more complex sentence structure, and more ideas per page than modern books. Recently written books, by contrast, use watered-down language and weaker, less complex sentence structures. If they have any meaningful ideas, they either sandwich them between pages and pages of fluff, or they club the reader over the head with the message.

In his introduction to *On the Incarnation* by Saint Athanasius, C. S. Lewis advises that moderns needed to read more old books and fewer new books. He explains:

> Every age has its own outlook. It is specially good at seeing certain truths and specially liable to make certain mistakes. We all, therefore, need the books that will correct the characteristic mistakes of our own period. And that means the old books. All contemporary writers share to some extent the contemporary outlook—even those, like myself, who seem most opposed to it.... To be sure, the books of the future would be just as good a corrective as the books of the past, but unfortunately we cannot get at them. (pp. 6–7)

We can see the blind spots of previous generations, but it is harder to know our own. Older books that we use have stood the test of time. They have been read for generations and will be read for generations more. It's too early to tell which of our currently published, modern crops of books will still be communicating to readers outside of the culture and time that produced them a hundred years from now. Authors' contemporaries are the worst judges of that timeless quality because we cannot step outside our own time, culture, and assumptions to see which are merely passing whims and which are timeless—not with any certainty, anyway.

The marginalizing of old books as though truth and beauty have expiration dates reflects modernity's disconnect with the past. A sense of the past is not just a matter of knowing dates and events and being able to put them in order. It's about coming into contact with some of the best minds of the previous centuries, not mere decades. It's about reading their ideas and stories in their words and getting a feel for truth, justice, mercy, faith, friendship, charity, loyalty, and courage. These are ideas and traits that are timeless.

While Mason did use some books which were newly published in her day, she relied more heavily on great books of the past. In *A Philosophy of Education*, she explains that the children read literature which was published in the same historical time period they are studying. She mentions Milton, Pope, Sir Walter Scott, Goldsmith—and of course, they were not modern in her day, either.

She explains:

> The object of children's literary studies is not to give them precise information as to who wrote what in the reign of whom?—but to give them a sense of the spaciousness of the days, not only of great Elizabeth, but of all those times of which poets, historians and the makers of tales, have left us living pictures. In such ways the children secure, not the sort of information which is of little cultural value, but wide spaces wherein imagination may take those holiday excursions deprived of which life is dreary; judgment, too, will turn over these folios of the mind and arrive at fairly just decisions about a given strike, the question of Poland, Indian Unrest. Every

> man is called upon to be a statesman seeing that every man and woman, too, has a share in the government of the country; but statesmanship requires imaginative conceptions, formed upon pretty wide reading and some familiarity with historical precedents. (p. 184)

It is not that her students never read modern books for literature; it's just that Mason did not see a need to emphasize them. She wrote that sometimes the oldest students' studies touched on "current literature in the occasional use of modern books; but young people who have been brought up on this sort of work may, we find, be trusted to keep themselves *au fait* with the best that is being produced in their own days" (p. 184).

It is also true that something we at AO appreciate about older books is that they are in the public domain. Many, many public domain books are still twaddle, so that alone won't qualify a book for AO. But once we've found a really well-written book, we love it when it's also public domain. This means they are available online as e-texts and *will remain available.* I can't tell you how frustrating it is, how much gnashing of teeth it causes the Advisory when a book goes out of print. When we put together the curriculum (and when we revise it), it was and is the result of truly thousands of Mama-hours (these are worth more than man-hours, right? Just joking!) researching books.

We have amazed our librarians with the number of books we checked out from the library and put on interlibrary loan. When all else fails, we actually (gulp) spend money on a book if we can't find it to review it any other way. We scan excerpts of different books into our computers and pass them on to each other to compare and contrast. We look at the wording, the breadth and scope of coverage, the illustrations (if any), and the topics covered (and just as important, topics not covered). Then, after devoting months of our lives to this project, we finally pick the best book of all those available and proudly and gleefully share it with the world. Then it goes out of print, and there is the aforesaid weeping and wailing and gnashing of teeth. Seriously, though, the newer, in-print books have a very high turnover rate. They quickly become hard-to-find and out-of-print books and thus of no use to us.

Individual homeschoolers can use and benefit from those books, of course. Some of them may actually be better than any given book we have listed. But a book that may be perfect for your family (or mine) is not perfect for AmblesideOnline if it's out of print but not online. Here are some reasons why out-of-print but not-yet-in-public-domain books are not very useful to us:

We want to share our vision of what a Charlotte Mason education might look like put into practice. At the same time, we want to make that vision available to as many people as possible who might want to benefit from it.

We specifically want to consider the unique situations and needs of missionaries, military, and other expat families overseas, as well as parents and educators around the world who love their kids; single parents; families without access to a decent library, a good bookstore, or inexpensive shipping; families who travel often and so cannot cart thousands of pounds of books around; and fellow homeschoolers all over the world.

We want to recreate a solid, sound, and beautiful rendition of what a C.M. curriculum might look like today, and we want that version to work for all those different families I mentioned. The best way for us to do that is to rely strongly on public domain works that can be used as e-texts, whenever we find e-texts of excellent quality.

This is not the only way to implement Charlotte Mason's ideas and principles. These are not the only books worth using. But these are the books that best fit the criteria we set for ourselves at the start of this project. We want to offer a model of what a real living book looks like. We want to share a curriculum based on excellently written books, packed with informing ideas rather than twaddle and barren facts, in living language that engages the mind (often with some effort required, which is also an important part of a C.M. education). So we have chosen what we believe to be the cream of the crop from those books that are online or still in print and, in some cases, worked hard to get that out-of-print book available online or convinced a publisher to republish.

We share this freely, and we try to keep costs down because we believe in Miss Mason's vision of "Education for all."

(*2016 post from* Archipelago)

## Karen: What Do I Do When My Child Doesn't Remember?

A lot of times, I hear AmblesideOnline / Charlotte Mason moms lament, "What do I do when my child doesn't remember?"

Maybe children don't narrate well at the time, and maybe they don't recall much about a topic later. We all hear the lovely stories and testimonials about the amazing connections that other children are making. What about the child for whom things don't seem to stick? Who doesn't remember?

You probably aren't going to like the answer, but...that's the way it's supposed to be. It took me a while to come to terms with this too, so I sympathize with your reluctance to accept this idea. Who follows an educational method that expects children to forget? And narration is supposed to help with remembering, so surely the children are expected to remember?

They won't forget everything, of course, but in a Charlotte Mason education, remembering a lot of specific information is simply not the object.

Our first hint that this is the case is actually found in the twelfth principle:

> "Education is the Science of Relations"; that is, that a child has natural relations with a vast number of things and thoughts: so we must train him upon physical exercises, nature, handicrafts, science and art, and upon *many living books*; for we know that our business is, not to teach him all about anything, but to help him make valid, as many as may be of [what Wordsworth called]

> "Those first born affinities, / That fit our new existence to existing things." (*A Philosophy of Education*, p. xxx)

In other words, education is the science of relations, and relationship trumps information in our educational endeavors.

One day, I was happily reading through *A Philosophy of Education*, when I was arrested by this paragraph:

> Education is a life. That life is sustained on ideas. Ideas are of spiritual origin, and God has made us so that we get them chiefly as we convey them to one another, whether by word of mouth, written page, Scripture word, musical symphony; but we must sustain a child's inner life with ideas as we sustain his body with food. Probably he will reject nine-tenths of the ideas we offer, as he makes use of only a small proportion of his bodily food, rejecting the rest. He is an eclectic; he may choose this or that; our business is to supply him with due abundance and variety and his to take what he needs. (p. 109)

My mind suddenly reshaped that word-fraction, nine-tenths, into a percentage: *90 percent.*

Probably he will reject *90 percent* of the ideas we offer. If you flip that around, probably he will accept and remember *only* 10 percent of the ideas we offer.

Those are some staggering numbers—they'd represent failure on graded tests. This is what Charlotte Mason is offering us? But passing tests isn't the point of education in this paradigm. Our object is to "sustain a child's inner life," and the only way that can happen is if he is offered an abundance and allowed to take what he needs. Charlotte Mason tells us that children hang the facts they remember on the ideas they take in, so if they are taking in only 10 percent of the ideas, they are also likely to remember only a portion of the associated facts.

If you want to educate your children using Charlotte Mason's philosophy, the wisest thing you can do is embrace this concept. Your children are learning, but they are learning in a relational way, not a remember-all-the-facts way.

> It is a great thing to possess a pageant of history in the background of one's thoughts. We may not be able to recall this or that circumstance, but, "the imagination is warmed"; we know that there is a great deal to be said on both sides of every question and are saved from crudities in opinion and rashness in action. The present becomes enriched for us with the wealth of all that has gone before. (*A Philosophy of Education*, p. 178)

It is very easy to lay hold of the idea that "it is a great thing to possess a pageant of history in the background of one's thoughts" and gloss over the uncomfortable truth that "we may not be able to recall this or that circumstance." If we are honest with ourselves, we'll admit that we would, indeed, like our children to be able to recall "this or that circumstance." And sometimes they do. But often they do not. In either case, we have laid the foundation of that pageant, warmed their imaginations, and enriched them by exposing them to the wealth of all that has gone before. This is true even if they can't remember a single king from *Our Island Story*.

Along the same lines, parents often lament that a child doesn't understand some things, and they feel compelled to explain. This is a fine practice if the child has requested an explanation but something to forego if he has not.

In a very useful pamphlet shared with a group of PNEU schools (*Notes for the Conference of July 18, 1925 on P.N.E.U. Methods* by H. W. Household), quite a severe warning is given about the practice.

> There are teachers who are not happy until they have made certain that there is not a line, not a word, that the child does not understand. Of course they are wrong. They are wasting time and hindering the child. The child has many years before [him], and [he] has [his] own times and ways of arriving at understanding. Next year, without our having said one word, [he] will understand much that [he] does not to-day. Let [him] do [his] own work upon the books. (pp. 9–10)

He underscores this point by emphasizing that "it is not expected that the children will grasp everything."

Viewed correctly, this should take a huge burden from the shoulders of the Charlotte Mason teacher. We should not expect children to grasp (or even remember) everything. We should expect something else; and if we understand the philosophy behind the educational methods we are following, we know what that is. Children are born persons. Education is the science of relations. We're going to give children every opportunity to form relationships with a wide variety of knowledge. We're going to ask them to narrate and tell us about the things they read and hear. And then we're going to get out of the way and let them go about the business of apprehending that 10 percent that is going to become a permanent possession for them.

Looking back on my own school days, I cannot remember one thing that I learned in second grade—not one. I do remember that on some days, I was allowed to leave the classroom and be a helper in the kindergarten room. That responsibility—I felt so important—I do remember. I don't remember a single thing I learned in fifth grade either, but I remember that my teacher read *The Hobbit* aloud to us, and I loved the story, so I borrowed the book from the library to read for myself (faster). My snippets represent less than 10 percent of what my teachers must have tried to teach me. Presumably I learned enough to move on to the next grade. But the bits that are a possession to me, many decades later, are the things that warmed my imagination and caught my heart.

It will be the same for your children. Read the books together. Narrate to each other; it's a relationship-building activity. Take joy in the 10 percent that your child pockets as a personal treasure and be willing to accept that the other 90 percent isn't what he needs right now. When your child doesn't remember, the right response is not to go back and retrace the same ground. Instead, go forward so that your child can find new ideas—the ones that will enrich his soul and sustain his inner life.

(*2018 post from* Archipelago)

# Snippet 2

**Lynn:**

On any given day, I suspect I have Charlotte spinning in her grave. True confessions: Our version of composer study for this week was me demonstrating to Justin that drumming is a *human art* and not something that can be satisfactorily provided by a drum machine, as is the case with much of the music he hears. I needed him to hear the difference and understand why I am unimpressed with so much of what passes for "great" in his generation. Examples I provided included Copeland—as in Stewart, not Aaron—with "Walking on the Moon" by The Police, Phil Collins' "In the Air Tonight," Paul Simon's *Graceland* tracks with the amazing South African musicians . . . and next week it just might be seventies funk (Clyde Stubblefield!) and Charlie Watts of the Rolling Stones. Ahem. I suspect this would not amuse C.M. purists, but it is, er, relevant.

But back on topic.

I also noticed in passing some mention of a Texas conference. Anybody know what that is about?

(*Email, 2015*)

# A Life of Rich Relationships

AmblesideOnline's free Charlotte Mason homeschool curriculum prepares children for a life of rich relationships with God, humanity, and the natural world. (AO website)

Once we see that we are dealing spirit with spirit with the friend at whose side we are sitting, with the people who attend to our needs, we shall be able to realise how incessant is the commerce between the divine Spirit and our human spirit. It will be to us as when one stops one's talk and one's thoughts in the springtime, to find the world full of bird-music unheard the instant before. (*Parents and Children,* pp. 276–277)

# Anne: The Indiana File

On a hot summer afternoon in Indiana, I stood at the front of a church sanctuary and gave a talk on "The Habit of Living Books" to the friends of AmblesideOnline who had gathered there for a weekend retreat.

I hadn't expected to be doing that.

What I had prepared wasn't planned to be a standing-on-the-stage talk. It was meant to be a sitting-in-a-small-room breakout session, but the sanctuary was the only space available, and even as a breakout presenter I was filling in at the last minute for someone else. I was in a time-zone-confusion fog, my watch had gotten misplaced at the bottom of my suitcase, and now there wasn't a clock where I could see one.

It wasn't that I had nothing to say. I had just finished writing my first book, *Minds More Awake*, and my thought-wheels were still spinning around that. And it wasn't that I was horrified by the idea of talking to a room full of people; I'd done that before. However, the surreal aspects, the unexpected changes, and the lack of a clock all combined to create a talk which went way overtime and afterward seemed something best forgotten.

A few years later I started working on a sequel to *Minds More Awake*. The Charlotte Mason educational world seemed to be both deepening and widening. New books and periodicals had appeared; new arrows were drawn to important and neglected points about narration and the value of physical objects. I thought I knew where I wanted to go with my own book.

And then I reopened my Indiana File. I approached it like a snake nut can, a bit afraid of what might pop out. This is one of the first things I saw:

> Much of what I am going to say today has already been said by Charlotte Mason, and I know most of you already know a lot about living books. But it doesn't hurt to go over some of the basics. It seems to me that a lot of it can be found right in the quotation from *Parents and Children* on the front of your retreat folders: "We find that children lay hold of all knowledge which is fitly presented to them with avidity, and therefore we maintain that a wide and generous curriculum is due to them" (p. 232).

I suddenly had the feeling that the woman rambling at the podium was more centered on C.M. principles than I had given her credit for and that she had a few things to pass on to the person I had become. This chapter is not that talk, but like the Indiana event itself, it gave me a beginning.

## Fellow Travelers

When I was a little girl, I wanted to be a teacher when I grew up (like my favorite miniskirted first-grade teacher). As I got older, I taught Sunday school, volunteered here and there, and took college courses in children's literature and psychology. I majored in something else entirely but nevertheless ended up teaching my own children at home for almost two decades. During those years, I discovered that I enjoyed working with adult groups, such as homeschooling parents and church classes, better than I liked teaching children (no offense to my kids). There seemed to be as much need for C.M. principles in the world of adults as there was in that of children.

Eventually, I started taking classes in adult education, doing my term papers on topics such as senior citizens' reasons for reading and what is happening to our reading lives in the digital age. I discovered that I could, so to speak, be a tour guide without having to pose as a so-called expert—that it was enough to walk alongside someone as a fellow traveler. Much adult educational theory reflected the way we, as Charlotte Mason educators, had approached the teaching of our own children—for instance, that adults without much formal schooling are individuals with valuable life experiences who are responsible for their own learning. All those nature walks where we asked them to look for themselves and all those times when we allowed them enough time to think and when we let them tell us what was in the painting instead of the other way around—we were learning something for ourselves as well and, more, something *about* ourselves.

## Don't Stop Interrupting

> Bronson Alcott, Louisa May Alcott's father, spoke of an education that opens out of the soul; we might also say opens out the soul, and again this is something we don't stop doing after we finish school or after our children finish school. (The Indiana File)

Sometime during my adult education program, I picked up a book called *Intentional Interruption*, which reminds teachers not to stop learning. The fact that such a thing needs to be written at all is a sad commentary on the state of education. However, I was struck by one startlingly honest point made in it: we (people in general, adults in particular, teachers not excepted) are not truly eager to learn. Learning requires change in thoughts and actions. Learning *is* change, or interruption, or unlearning. And that produces discomfort. Children may "lay hold with avidity," but the rest of us can usually find a reason to avoid having to carve out a new brain-track. In the Gospels, there are probably more accounts of people being made uncomfortable and saying "later" or "no" than there are of instant disciples.

Charlotte recognized our tendency to choose the default mode, almost from the beginning of her teaching career. In her nineteenth principle of education, she mentions the "loose thinking and heedless action which cause most of us to live at a lower level than we need" (*A Philosophy of Education*, p. xxxi). But after we agree that it is high time to live sanely and to pursue learning that opens out our souls, and after we have determined to bypass the usual traps and dead ends, how do we begin? Are we willing to be interrupted?

*Intentional Interruption* says that when we do decide there is room for improvement, we tend to go after it in all the wrong ways, trying to solve too many problems at once, or chasing after side issues, or blindly copying someone else's program of change without understanding why those ideas worked for them or how we could adapt them for our own context. Perhaps, like a story told in the book about a sudden fad for teachers to sit on exercise balls (because one admired teacher happened to find it comfortable), we adopt a surface feature of a successful method, then wonder why we do not get the wonderful results we expected.

The problem may also be one of our unwillingness to commit ourselves fully to one idea, to stay on the narrow road without looking for shortcuts and bypasses. *Pilgrim's Inn* is the second book of the Eliot Family trilogy written by Elizabeth Goudge. The British title for the novel was *The Herb of Grace*, which refers to rue, a bitter herb that is the source of our word *rue*, or regret. It's mentioned several times in the book, and discussed outright as a symbol of astringency, meaning contraction or pulling back. The first time I read it, I was confused by the herb analogy; but now I see the point that allowing ourselves to be constricted, or pulled a little tighter, is like realizing that we can't have everything—that having the ability to choose means that sometimes we have to say "No."

A recent online discussion mentioned the nebulous concept of "Relaxed Charlotte Mason" (to differentiate it from "Uptight Charlotte Mason"?). Again, it's a term that leaves the door ajar. If you say "C.M. all the way," you're committing yourself, and that's uncomfortable. You might be watched and graded on your C.M.-ness. People also avoid saying, "I follow Charlotte Mason's methods" because they feel it might sound judgmental, boastful, or like Charlotte-Mason-worship. "Eclectic Homeschooling" and "Relaxed Charlotte Mason" just sound friendlier. But Charlotte herself scolded people about being falsely modest, too polite, or squeamish about sharing their beliefs. If you discover something to be true, it isn't arrogant to stand by it. It's about the truth of the idea itself, not about how smart you are to see it.

## Is there a "Mere C.M.?"

> ...and studying the subjects we do cover with books, real books—with real things as well, but largely with real books, inspiring real ideas and real questions, modeling real vocabulary, awakening real curiosity, offering real mind-food. (The Indiana File)

The problem with trying to describe a Charlotte Mason education is that like the proverbial elephant, we must begin by taking hold of one part, say an ear, and risk ignoring, or at least risk appearing to ignore, the tail and legs and trunk. Asked to lead an information session or write a synopsis, some begin with a biography of the person and the movement. Others choose phrases such as "Education is the science of relations," "Habit is ten natures," "I am, I can, I ought, I will"; or a practical aspect, such as nature study or notebook-keeping; or something that inspired Mason, such as the fresco in a chapel. The interesting thing is that any of these parts lead to what we should call the body of the elephant: a deep, classically inspired understanding of education as the formation of character, all under the guidance of the Holy Spirit.

If we're going to choose metaphors, though, I prefer the image of a tree, whose trunk can be accessed not only from the large branches of principles and practices but also from the twigs. My personal twigs have included *Pilgrim's Progress*, the names of clouds, the poetry of T.S. Eliot, fast and slow fashion, and the dinner parties of Plutarch—not to mention fellow explorers waving from further down the trunk or from their own branches. All have drawn me back to the trunk of a few central points.

First, abundance. Things and books. We don't discount the things, but we also can't do this without books. Lots of books and the right kind of books—a rich, varied, generous idea-serving. For those of us who presume to teach, the "limited measure" of our minds is less important than our commitment to "abundant provision and orderly serving" (*A Philosophy of Education*, p. 26). However, we sometimes mistake abundant serving for piling the plate beyond a child's appetite. Our confident parent-teacher demeanor may still be troubled by gaps and blank spaces, especially in a culture full of baby flashcards and standardized testing. We are quick to lay out money for curriculum that promises to cover everything.

The classic example of piling in my homeschooling years was an overstuffed timeline binder, rivaling medieval Bibles in weight. We thought that's what a Book of Centuries must be, and we wanted to do it right. But that particular error was turned on its head several years ago by C.M. educator and researcher Laurie Bestvater, author of *The Living Page*. She discovered that the original Book of Centuries was a relatively thin notebook, with quite small spaces to record events. The notebook was designed in that way to allow students to experience the power of prioritizing and choosing. It taught them to view knowledge as a wide mesh in which gaps were natural and accepted but in which there was always the possibility of filling in a little here, a little there. Like a carry-on suitcase, the key to using it was to choose its contents carefully—not so much to regret what it could not contain as to appreciate what it could. We might say that its rediscovery symbolized our need to better understand astringency.

## Little by Little

> *"Education is the science of relations..."* (Charlotte Mason's twelfth principle)

The second essential component in education is relations, which implies something far removed from randomness, fragmentation, and what Charlotte called scraps of knowledge. From efforts to teach tiny children sustained play, to insistence on full attention in the schoolroom, to the reading of whole books rather than excerpts, to musings on adult service and citizenship, this thread can be followed throughout her writings. It flies in the face of current-day enthusiasm for disconnected facts, sidebars, and nonlinear texts.

Part of the value of a long-term relationship with books is in the overall building up of skill and strength, along with what we learn from each book. It is not necessarily in seeing exciting moments all the time, not always in something you may be able to point to and say, "We're there." In *How to Read a Book*, Mortimer J. Adler and Charles Van Doren say that high-level reading goes beyond the "inspectional" and "analytical" stages and moves into "syntopical" reading—a stage of fluency where we are ready to compare the ideas we have gathered from various sources and, in whatever way we are able, to join in the discussion (pp. 16–20). This echoes Charlotte's insistence that "we must teach children to choose between the ideas that present themselves, which is the one responsible work of a human being" (*Parents and Children*, p. 230).

So we recognize that "mere C.M." includes using time well (neither rushing nor dawdling), serving up lessons in an orderly (non-fragmented) way, and building up learning muscle along with character. The question of following strict schedules in the C.M. classroom is a thorny one, especially in the homeschool context where, unlike many households of Charlotte's era, our children do not arrive promptly in a dedicated schoolroom for lessons with the governess but often find their schoolwork stretched over, around, and through the rest of family life. Many of us have encouraged our older children to take responsibility for their own learning, including managing their study schedules, chores, and so on; it would seem like a backward step to tell them when to start and when to close the book. In addition, a number of homeschoolers are those who did not or would not do well in the typical structure of a classroom or whose days at home are unpredictable due to medical situations or other needs. What are we C.M. purists to do?

It seems there are basic principles (or natural laws) that govern nearly everything, not just education; and making the effort to understand them will help us decide how and when to apply them. In the case of the oldest ones, we might look at the guidance given in *Formation of Character*, in the chapters concerning the "young maidens at home," such as this:

> The woman who has herself well in hand, who thinks her own thoughts, reserves her judgments, considers her speech, controls her actions—she is the woman who succeeds in life, with a success to be measured by her powers of heart, brain, and soul. (p. 238)

The goal is to have oneself "well in hand," no matter whether the parent or the student devises the schedule, and to plan for the day's work, accommodating changes but resisting unnecessary distractions. Younger ones will need more time guidance, but the goals are the same: accepting that one's Ought at any time is to carry out the activity, no matter how small, which is set for that time, and to keep at it with full attention until it is done properly. Again: astringency.

Charlotte's philosophy also puts a great deal of emphasis on seeing things in their context. In *Herbartian Psychology* (a book she mentions), Sir John Adams talks about the mistaken idea that we can learn information from the top down—that is, reading the dictionary and then looking for objects that match the vocabulary list rather than first meeting those things where they live and then finding out their names and where they fit into the big picture. Education through building up relations is not the same as opening one magic book that is going to give us all the answers or swallowing a pill containing everything we need to know. It's more like gradually writing our own dictionaries or encyclopedias, building from the bottom up.

It seems to me that we try to teach many things top down, often wasting a great deal of time in the process. Sometimes that happens because a subject is familiar to us as adults and we forget that children haven't yet made the same connections. Sometimes we learned things ourselves without knowing that there *is* a context—a thought that might encourage us to explore mathematics history, or to learn what other musical scales existed before Western music settled on do-re-mi, or to find out how something we take for granted is handled in another culture. Something as simple as reading a chapter in the book where it belongs (rather than in an anthology or a reader) is a way to meet things where they live. In the same way, moving on from one historical event to another whenever possible also provides a context that should be natural but all too often is missing.

One may argue that young children have little sense of time and geography, citing their funny questions about whether Grandma ever met Noah as evidence. Certainly, young students can enjoy *Little House in the Big Woods* without fully understanding how many years ago Laura was born or who was president at that time. As a young child, I remember reading an old book about a family traveling on some adventure or other, and I assumed that they did so in a car like my father's chrome-heavy Chevrolet rather than a

Tin Lizzie or a horse and buggy. If they had had to crank the car or the horse had run away, I might have noticed; but it didn't make any difference to the way that story turned out.

Another example of the need to be patient about this is the reaction of parents reading Charlotte Yonge's *The Little Duke*. They almost invariably start worrying about how to explain the family connection between Duke Richard and his great-grandson William the Conqueror, or was that his great-great-grandson? In the early years, it's not being scrappy to focus on the story itself, with just a bit of this-came-first, then-this. In geography, it's fine to explain that the city where our cousins live is quite close to us and we can drive there in an hour but when we go to another city to visit friends, the journey takes two days and we have to stop somewhere to sleep. In fact, it is the books themselves and the paintings, the musical compositions, the short and long journeys, and the outdoor adventures, that will provide a foundation for the later, more specific understanding of time and distance.

## Adequate, Necessary, and Speaking to Our Time

> That system which shall be of use to practical people in giving purpose, unity and continuity to education, must satisfy the following demands:—*It must be adequate*, covering the whole nature of man and his relations with all that is other than himself. *It must be necessary*, that is, no other equally adequate psychology should present itself; and *it must touch at all points the living thought of the age*. (*School Education*, p. 46)

A C.M. education is not utilitarian, but it must be practical. "Practical" often means completing arithmetic worksheets, singing spelling-rule songs, and learning useful things like the capital cities of Canada, not traipsing through the woods and memorizing lines from Shakespeare. Or it might mean hands-on activities involving glue, measuring cups, or plastic counting shapes. But the root meaning of the word *practical* is more closely related to the principles of conduct, particularly as they are *acted* upon, *practiced*. The goals are, as Charlotte says in *Ourselves*, using the lessons gained and the examples modeled to build up one's conscience so that wise, loving, and just decisions can be made and acted upon. Like Robert Frost, we understand that we can't go down every road, but we are satisfied to know that our own path has a purpose. Again: astringency.

## Procuring the Treasure

> Charlotte Mason said that the initiation of ideas will develop the habits of thought and feeling. So, another reason for using living books: to help children become more aware of feelings such as reverence, pleasure, admiration, appreciation, awe. We need to encourage awe and wonder, the idea that there is meaning to things beyond our own uses for things. (The Indiana File)

The German word *sehnsucht*, a favourite of C.S. Lewis, means "longing for completion" (or, as Lewis put it, for joy). I thought of this recently when I had to pause an online activity to watch a commercial for a jigsaw puzzle app. Watching the virtual finger steadily putting virtual pieces together inside a virtual frame felt both calming and annoying. I traced the annoyance to a feeling that had nothing to do with the finger or the app: "If only things could be that simple." The puzzle of life does not always fit together so beautifully. Sometimes, to our frustration, we have just completed a whole section when suddenly it seems those pieces have become irrelevant, and we must begin again.

However, it is the image of continuing to build up our picture—extending it outside the original frame if necessary—that is most useful as an image of an ongoing education, fired by our human longing to find and reconnect scattered pieces. What is the treasure that, though hidden and dusty, is there waiting for us to claim it and own it? "The best thought the world possesses," wrote Charlotte, "is stored in books" (*A Philosophy of Education*, p. 26). We can trust in the books themselves and in the children's natural desire for knowledge. Focusing on the substance of the book—the content, the ideas, and not so much the mechanics of teaching—makes the whole thing suddenly much simpler. Then we need to use it in a way that makes use of all the habits and skills, intelligence and imagination, powers of attention and observation that are already in our children.

## One Reading to Bind Them

I've learned to discount the idea that "Charlotte Mason" is something that appeals to a certain bookish sort of teacher and student and that therefore, if you can't visualize your children sitting still for tea and poetry, or ever sitting still at all, you had better move on rather quickly to another booth at the homeschool conference. I'm not trying to equate educational philosophy with faith, but it seems to me that that idea is akin to saying you should pick your religious beliefs according to your personality. As an introvert you might prefer a small fellowship, or as someone with a love of baroque music you might choose to worship in a cathedral with a pipe organ; but those things are not the same as saying that Christianity appeals only to certain personality types and the rest should check out another pathway altogether. The same principle applies to educational truths.

> The solid-seeming earth on which you stand is but a heaving bubble, bursting ever and anon in this place and in that. Only above all, and through all, and with all, is One who does not move nor change, but is the same yesterday, today, and forever. And on Him, and not on this bubble of an earth, do you and I, and all of

> us, depend. (Charles Kingsley, *Madam How and Lady Why*, p. 53)

This is closely related to the problem of retired homeschooling mothers who no longer feel they fit in at meetings and conferences. If discussions are only about phonics, arithmetic, and how to keep the toddler from destroying the bookshelves, that makes perfect sense. But if we are educating our children to develop character; to build relationships with God, people, and the universe; and to instill the habits of a lifetime, then we are doing no less for ourselves. That isn't something we can drop when we no longer have someone narrating on the couch beside us. Charlotte's books cover everything from infant care to the vocational thoughts of young adults and the musings of headmasters, not to mention all the points she draws from literary characters (such as in *Formation of Character*). The only life stage about which she doesn't say much is the senior years; perhaps if she had written a seventh volume, it might have been called *Retirement-Home Education.*

> It is not the friends of our election who have exclusive claims upon us; the friends brought to us here and there by the circumstances of life all claim our loyalty, and from these we get ...kindness for kindness, service for service, loyalty for loyalty, full measure, heaped together and running over. (*Ourselves*, book II, p. 32)

For over twenty years, some of my closest fellow travelers have been C.M. colleagues, particularly the members of the AO Advisory and its Auxiliary. Tolkien wrote about the Fellowship of the Ring, Wendell Berry about the Port William Membership. But I prefer the way that St. Paul described Epaphroditus: we have become companions in labour and fellow soldiers (Philippians 2:25). From the start, we believed that we were brought into a job that we were called to see through together. In that sense, we have met Charlotte's goal of objectivity while also enjoying the growth of an irreplaceable friendship.

Does this sound too exclusive? Too astringent?

I did not think so when I stood on the podium in Indiana, and at later events in Texas and Tennessee, and looked out at the faces of our fellow soldiers, many of whom have shown us "kindness for kindness, service for service, loyalty for loyalty." Tolkien's hobbit Frodo might have shared his deepest (and darkest) experiences with Sam, Merry, and Pippin; but he was also a citizen of the Shire, and his ring-bearing quest was for all of them. Charlotte said, "As things are we shall have to see to it that everybody gets fed"—simply meeting the basic needs, "but our hope is that henceforth we shall bring up our young people with self-sustaining minds, as well as self-sustaining bodies, by a due ordering of the process of education. We hope so to awaken and direct mind hunger that every man's mind will look after itself" (*A Philosophy of Education*, p. 281). This was a long-term plan—something she imagined as just getting rolling but moving along on its own in the future. What she hoped for, if this idea of a living education took root, was that all kinds of people—wealthy people, working people—would become reading people.

But if we are going to discuss hobbits, it is Sam's story that speaks the closest to our Advisory hearts. Galadriel had given Sam, the gardener, a little box containing a silver nut and some earth from her orchard, with the promise that "Though you should find all barren and laid waste, there will be few gardens in Middle-earth that will bloom like your garden, if you sprinkle this earth there" (*The Fellowship of the Ring*, J.R.R. Tolkien, p. 486). In his work to restore the ruined Shire, Sam plants the nut, and also many saplings, each fertilized with a bit of the earth ("the precious dust"). Finally, he goes as close to the center of the Shire as he can and casts the last bit of earth into the air, with a blessing that is fulfilled many times over in the next harvest.

Each of the Advisory families has taken on both the planting of the AO nut and the tending of its own saplings. Strangely, it is the random tossing of the last few grains that has cost us the most but has also brought the greatest blessing. Because this is real life, not a Middle-earth fantasy, some of our own plantings did not flourish in quite the ways we envisioned; and we wondered sometimes whether we should have hoarded a few extra bits for ourselves. But, as Charlotte said, children are born persons, not bonsai trees or exhibits for a flower show. Growth (as we know ourselves) is not ultimately measured on graduation day but continues throughout our lives.

We have also seen the blessing of sending AO freely out into places we couldn't have dreamed of—to people who have taken it and used it to teach their own children and those of others and now also to the first seedlings of the second generation. Galadriel's gift was meant to be shared freely and in faith, and in that I think we have succeeded.

## Karen: Trust the Process

Can you go back in your mind to that period of time when your oldest was only five or six or seven and you were just beginning your homeschool journey? It's such a weight of responsibility we take on, and I don't blame anyone for getting overwhelmed with trying to find *exactly* the right thing because so much (it seems) is riding on the curriculum we choose. I remember being overwhelmed by curriculum fairs back in the 1990s, and I think it must be even more overwhelming now. Back then, homeschoolers had yet to become a market. There were lots of good choices, but how can you be sure—absolutely sure—that you are choosing the right thing?

Charlotte Mason's methods and philosophy are *so* satisfying and freeing if you understand what is behind them. Her extended metaphor of the mind as a living organism that needs to be fed gives us so much to ponder. It exactly answers this quandary. Your children need a healthy diet. You have a working knowledge of nutritional needs. You offer protein, vegetables, fruits, and grains at regular intervals and with some kind of balance. You serve meals on a regular basis, and you make sure that the quantities are adequate. There is room for snacks, but you know that too much low-quality junk food will interfere with your children's appetite for healthy food.

Does it matter if you have breakfast at 7:30 or 9:00? Does it matter if you have peanut butter for lunch all the time? Does it matter if you eat a predictable round of casseroles or experiment with lots of ethnic recipes? Not really. If the basic ingredients are healthy and there is enough variety and quantity, it will nourish your children and they will grow. Providing that menu and offering it up is *all* you can do. You cannot chew, swallow, or digest a thing for your children. They must eat for themselves.

In education, Charlotte Mason has told us what the healthy diet is—ideas. She has shown us that children have a healthy appetite for all kinds of ideas, all across the curriculum. Your job is to serve it up, but you can no more force your child to learn than you can force him to digest. All such force-feeding is spewed out of the mind, forgotten, eliminated without digestion or nourishment. Charlotte Mason urges us to provide a wide and generous curriculum. This is a *principle*—the violation of which means we will not reap the benefits of her methods.

But you know what? You don't have to use her recipe for potatoes or pot roast or spaghetti. The recipes that Charlotte Mason used to make her principles work for the PNEU students are just one way of realizing the principles. Her timetables are guidelines, not *principles*. You do not hinder the benefits of the method if you find other ways to implement the principles. If your family prefers to do school in the afternoons or evenings because Dad works second shift and is home in the morning, that's okay. If you substitute a book or add in some Asian history because of your heritage, that's great. If your chosen foreign language is Polish because you happen to live in Poland, that's as it should be. There are twenty principles, which are the overarching guidelines that give shape and structure to our educational methods; but the details—the specific recipes for meat, veggies, fruits, and grains—can flex a great deal without harming the principles.

But how can you know that when your oldest is just starting out in homeschool? You really can't. You have to choose as wisely as you can and trust the process. Look at moms with older children who are well-grown and healthy. What are they doing? Will that work for you? Do you need to adapt? What kinds of adaptations will work? Stay in community, glean from the wisdom of others, and take comfort in the fact that you managed to keep your children physically fed so far, and you can feed them intellectually too. You can do this.

(*Posted on the AO Forum, 2017*)

# Lynn: A Magical Expansion

> "Education is the Science of Relations"; that is, that a child has natural relations with a vast number of things and thoughts: so we must train him upon physical exercises, nature, handicrafts, science and art, and upon *many living books*; for we know that our business is, not to teach him all about anything, but to help him make valid, as many as may be of [what Wordsworth called] "Those first born affinities, / That fit our new existence to existing things." (*A Philosophy of Education*, p. xxx)

## "Education is the Science of Relations."

This is a principle that you must see running about in muddy sneakers to fully understand.

My children were very young when I first read this phrase, and although at the time I thought I knew what the words meant, hindsight now winks at me. I suspect that only through living with children over a course of years does one come to apprehend this principle. As my little ones slid down from my lap and landed smack in a big wide world that needed full inspection, I began to see this principle with feet on—sometimes in those muddy sneakers, slogging in with sloshing jars of tadpoles, other times in sock feet on the sofa, mind-questing through worlds of words as I read aloud. Those feet never stopped running circles around me—I could scarcely run apace! And I began to see that my little explorers truly were educated best by the relationships they formed firsthand with all sorts of things—and people—in their world.

> The idea that vivifies teaching in the Parents' Union is that "Education is the Science of Relations;" by which phrase we mean that children come in to the world with a natural "appetancy," to use Coleridge's word, for, and affinity with, all the material of knowledge; for interest in the heroic past and in the age of myths; for a desire to know about everything that moves and lives, about strange places and strange peoples; for a wish to handle material and to make; a desire to run and ride and row and do whatever the law of gravitation permits. (*Parents and Children*, pp. 222–223)

## "...that is, that a child has natural relations with a vast number of things and thoughts..."

The meaning of life is found in our relationships—to people, ideas and creation. A life lived in a stupor of apathy and selfishness meets its empty end like the world in T.S. Eliot's "The Hollow Men"—"not with a bang, but with a whimper" (p. 92). The radius of a hollow life locks down on the dull, close borders of its own needs, with no relationship to anything or anyone. But when a person forms a relationship with something, it becomes a part of his consciousness, his being. And every relationship formed redefines and expands the mind, which makes his world a bit larger, his life fuller.

> On what does Fulness of Living depend?—What is education after all? An answer lies in the phrase—Education is the Science of Relations. I do not use this phrase, let me say once more, in the Herbartian sense—that things are related to each other, and we must be careful to pack the right things in together, so that, having got into the brain of a boy, each thing may fasten on its cousins, and together they may make a strong clique or "apperception

> mass." What we are concerned with is the fact that we personally have relations with all that there is in the present, all that there has been in the past, and all that there will be in the future—with all above us and all about us—and that fulness of living, expansion, expression, and serviceableness, for each of us, depend upon how far we apprehend these relationships and how many of them we lay hold of. George Herbert says something of what I mean—Man is all symmetry, Full of proportions, one limb to another, And *all to all the world besides*; Each part may call the farthest brother, For head with foot hath private amity, And *both with moons and tides*. Every child is heir to an enormous patrimony, heir to all the ages, inheritor of all the present. (*School Education*, pp.185–186)

To me, this principle speaks to the big question of life: Why are you here? You're born, you sojourn here a while, you die and go home to the Lord for all eternity. That part of our existence spent here on this little ball spinning around the sun is a mere pin-dot on the unfathomable timeline of eternity. So what is the point of being here? It's astounding that God created so much for so temporary a phase of our existence. Why didn't He just create us in heaven and skip this part?

There are, of course, larger issues in this question, which are beyond our scope here. But it is fair to say that God purposed for us to gain wisdom and understanding while here. To help us along in that regard, He created an infinitely fascinating world, full of learning opportunities. Paul writes in Romans that God is clearly revealed in the things He created. And all those created things were formed by the same Hand that made us—thus, we are related to everything that was made through the bond of our common Creator. This inherent relationship to all things is what Charlotte called affinities, which she illustrates in this principle with a phrase from Wordsworth's *The Prelude*: "those first-born affinities that fit our new existence to existing things." Perhaps the best we can do in this brief sojourn phase of our eternal existence is use our gifts ...enrich our affinities...by forming vital relationships with the things and people He created for us.

This, in insufficiently elegant terms, is the medieval philosophy of education. Charlotte found this philosophy compelling and reforming, returning to it again and again in the Series. She draws our attention to a complex and beautiful fresco in the Spanish Chapel in Florence that illuminates this philosophy. It so inspired her that she had a copy of it hung at Ambleside for all to study and meditate upon. Through her descriptions (such as that in *School Education*), we begin to glimpse the scope of the great banquet of affinities. Every subject represented on the fresco brings its own gifts to the human spirit. As Francis Bacon famously noted, "Histories make men wise; poets, witty; the mathematics, subtle; natural philosophy, deep; moral, grave; logic and rhetoric, able to contend."

## "...so we train him upon physical exercises, nature lore, handicrafts, science and art, and upon many living books..."

This is a full and generous curriculum, referring back to principle 11 and ahead to principle 13. But since curriculum particulars are not the focus of the present principle, Charlotte lists but a partial sampling so as not to distract us from the larger idea at hand. However, I can't help but note the nature of the subjects she chooses to illustrate this point—they are all beyond the scope of utilitarian and three Rs systems of education. Further, I take special notice of her deliberate inclusion of exercise and handicrafts. These are the only two areas that provide the child an opportunity to develop the very vital affinity for physical intelligence (as well as the wisdom to seek wholeness and refreshment in recreational activity). Ironically, they are the two areas we most often slight.

> Our part is to drop occasion freely in the way, whether in school or at home. Children should have relations with earth and water, should run and leap, ride and swim....He must stand and walk and run and jump with ease and grace. He must skate and swim and ride and drive, dance and row and sail a boat. (*School Education*, p. 209)

In exercise, the child not only profits physically but also absorbs the laws of nature and empathy with the experiences of other beings. Charlotte also points out that the child who is familiar with his physical abilities from much leaping and climbing is less apt to suffer injury from misjudging his physical limitations or to be bullied into foolish dares by his playmates. She encourages games such as cricket and tennis, which not only improve muscle strength and coordination but also strengthen character in that they exert the mind to act quickly within the limits of precise rules. And in a very carefully worded passage, Charlotte alludes to the importance of exercise in expending certain physical energies that beset older children.

All in all, Charlotte was beyond the thinking of her times in this very holistic view that mind, body, and spirit are inextricably fused together in effect toward overall health.

Neglect of handiwork also presents the child with many unnecessary future challenges that many busy parents fail to foresee. It's in handicrafts that a child forms an ease with many work-related skills—the use of tools, abstract planning processes, sequencing, problem-solving and so on. But perhaps more importantly, the pursuit of handicrafts provides the child a vital affinity for the satisfaction of productivity and thus the capacity to find joy and fulfillment in his own labors (see Ecclesiastes 2:24, 3:13, 3:22). Handicrafts teach a child to take joy in the virtue of being busy in a productive way—a most useful habit that will guide and serve him throughout life.

**"...for we know that our business is not to teach him all about anything, but to help him to make valid as many as may be of—'Those first-born affinities That fit our new existence to existing things.'"**

We cannot fully prepare a child for every demand of life and career, but Charlotte urges us to usher him toward an abundant life:

> In proportion to the range of living relationships we put in his way, will he have wide and vital interests, fulness of joy in living. In proportion as he is made aware of the laws which rule every relationship, will his life be dutiful and serviceable: as he learns that no relation with persons or with things, animate or inanimate, can be maintained without strenuous effort, will he learn the laws of work and the joys of work. (*School Education*, pp. 187–188)

She also desired that this broad enrichment of his "first-born affinities" in childhood would result in the highest realization of his God-given capacities throughout his life:

> In the great (and ungoverned) age of the Renaissance, the time when great things were done, great pictures painted, great buildings raised, great discoveries made, the same man was a painter, an architect, a goldsmith and a master of much knowledge besides; and all that he did he did well, all that he knew was part of his daily thought and enjoyment. (*A Philosophy of Education*, pp. 53–54)

Not just the great Renaissance man but all people, even common laborers, should be blessed with this "daily thought and enjoyment"—a lively storehouse of mind that lightens our daily toils:

> Only as he has been and is nourished upon books is a man able to "live his life." A great deal of mechanical labour is necessarily performed in solitude; the miner, the farm-labourer, cannot think all the time of the block he is hewing, the furrow he is ploughing; how good that he should be figuring to himself the trial scene in the *Heart of Midlothian*, the "high-jinks" in *Guy Mannering*, that his imagination should be playing with "Ann Page" or "Mrs. Quickly," or that his labour goes the better "because his secret soul a holy strain repeats." People, working people, do these things. Many a one can say out of rich experience, "My mind to me a kingdom is." (*A Philosophy of Education*, p. 331)

Herein we see the driving force behind Charlotte's life's work—that children have a divinely implanted capacity to develop their "first-born affinities" for knowledge into lifelong relationships.

For illustration of how this looks in muddy sneakers, so to speak, she quotes at great length from Ruskin's autobiographical *Praeterita* and Wordsworth's *The Prelude*. She urges all parents to read these two works and particularly admonishes "suburban dwellers of the rich middle class" (*School Education*, p. 190) to read Ruskin's book because his tales of struggling against the overprotective limitations imposed on his childhood show us, as parents, how not to do it. Childhood affinities stay with us through life, and perhaps beyond. Charlotte notes how bountifully they come to fruition in adulthood—Ruskin's childhood fascination for pebbles "resulted in the life-shaping intimacy with minerals to which we owe *Ethics of the Dust*" (*School Education*, p. 196). And of Sir Walter Scott, she writes, "Scott laid claim to 'intimacy with all ranks of my countrymen from the Scottish peer to the Scottish ploughman,' and—we get the Waverly novels" (*School Education*, p. 203). (Charlotte read from Scott's historical novels nightly, along with the Bible, throughout her life. When she finished them all, she would simply begin again.)

Examples from the modern era spring to mind. Sir Winston Churchill had two childhood fascinations—history stories and his toy soldiers, which he tirelessly arranged by era and rank and reenacted historical battles. As prime minister of Great Britain, he became one of the greatest statesmen in world history and was a major strategist in World War II. In his last years, he wrote many definitive volumes on world history. Likewise, as a child, General George Patton was transfixed by cavalry, particularly in the military career of Stonewall Jackson. He followed in Jackson's footsteps, becoming a brilliant tank commander—the modern equivalent of cavalry. In our own era, Homer Hickam's best-selling autobiographical novels relate how his boyhood fascination with homemade rockets paved the way for NASA's voyages to the moon and beyond.

Childhood affinities are powerful! How different the world could be if all children came to adulthood bountifully furnished with worthy relationships to draw upon and grow from for a lifetime.

> [Every] child should leave school with at least a couple of hundred pictures by great masters hanging permanently in the halls of his imagination, to say nothing of great buildings, sculpture, beauty of form and colour in things he sees. Perhaps we might secure at least a hundred lovely landscapes, too—sunsets, cloudscapes, star-light nights. At any rate he should go forth well furnished because imagination has the property of magical expansion, the more it holds the more it will hold. (*A Philosophy of Education*, p. 43)

We are inspired to provide a banquet of rich ideas, without predigestion or contrivance. Relationships are personal, not vicarious—we cannot form them for someone else. Years of living with those muddy sneakers have taught me that if I wallop my children with a prefabricated packet of facts and projects pertaining to, say, trees, they soon tire of it so that even a tree swing begins to lose its charm. Their zeal proves self-perpetuating, however, if I allow them to form those vital connections here a little and there a little. Gaps for pondering are essential—we need the grace of space, time to fit the new ideas to the relationship in progress.

Over time, things pertaining to trees will naturally surface across a variety of subjects. In handicrafts children can come to know the nature of wood—how it swells in water, how silky it feels when sanded, how it smells when sawed or burned, how it sounds hollow or solid, how it glows with polish and stain, how it responds to the pressure of a chisel, how splinters feel in the flesh. In science, they learn how the tree lives—how it sprouts, how it feeds through photosynthesis and drinks through the mirror of itself in the roots underground, how it colors through chlorophyll and climate, how it marks time through rings. They are awed by the majesty of a tree through the strokes of master artists and the ponderings of poets. Inspired by nature lore, they plant a seedling and cheer as it bolts beyond their own height. Trees become their friends for life.

As I grow older, I begin to see that, like the mind, knowledge also has the property of magical expansion. The more I learn, the more there seems to be yet to learn. As I begin to fathom how much I do not know—and thus how endless the mind of God is, I grow less certain that we can truly make knowledge belong to us. Knowledge predates us. In the sense that it all comes from God, it was here from the beginning. I note that Wordsworth took care to qualify that our existence is new and that our affinities fit us, in our newness, to existing things. We are materialistic by nature: we want to own things. Regardless, I begin to suspect that the relationships we form with knowledge do not make it belong to us but rather bring us to belong to what was here all along.

My father once said in a sermon, "We spend our lives preoccupied with the things that belong to us. We come to believe we are defined by those things, that they will give us joy. But in the end, it doesn't matter what belongs to you. What does matter? What defines who you are? What gives you joy? Only to what—and to whom—you belong."

This, for me, sums up "The Science of Relations"—belonging to, and richly enjoying, all those things to which God blessed us with first-born affinities.

> "Charge them that are rich in this world, that they be not high-minded, nor trust in uncertain riches, but in the living God, who giveth us richly all things to enjoy. (2 Timothy 6:17–19)

(*AO website*)

# Snippet 3

**Anne:**

C.S. Lewis had an epiphany about knowledge while standing in a dark toolshed. First, he looked at a beam of light coming in; then he looked along the beam and saw green leaves and sky through the crack where the light came in. He wrote an essay comparing that to two sorts of knowledge—a rational, analyzing sort and a sort of intelligence beyond that, a fragment of the way God sees things.

So, okay. I've heard this before. Both types of scholarship, or knowing, or seeing matter, and you can apply the idea to different things: theology, poetry, art, science. But I just thought: studying Charlotte Mason is like that too. We're often looking at the beam of light, or what she wrote—analyzing her words, talking about school and habits, discussing where she found such an idea. But other times, we sort of climb up on all that information and stand on tiptoe, looking through the cracks for what's beyond. This is why I think we've stuck with it past the young-mom schooling years.

Another way the two are distinguished: thinking about something vs. breathing it in. Again, both are necessary, but if you only stay on the thinking level and never get to the atmosphere, Narnian air, breathing part, you're missing out.

**Karen:**

It's as if Charlotte Mason is standing and gazing out at a wide vista of mountains, rivers, plains—beauty and knowledge only glimpsed, which a lifetime isn't enough to explore closely. And while she's talking about the wonderful things she sees, some folks are listening; but they are facing her instead of the vista—hearing what she's saying but missing the actual experience of seeing the expanse for themselves.

(*Emails, 2023*)

# The Bee-Loud Glade

*"The Lake Isle of Innisfree" has been a favorite Advisory poem for years. Lynn once described it this way: "It has endowed us with an archetype of a space where we can be together even though we are not."*

**The Lake Isle of Innisfree**

By William Butler Yeats

I will arise and go now, and go to Innisfree,

And a small cabin build there, of clay and wattles made;

Nine bean-rows will I have there, a hive for the honey bee,

And live alone in the bee-loud glade.

And I shall have some peace there, for peace comes dropping slow,

Dropping from the veils of the morning to where the cricket sings;

There midnight's all a glimmer, and noon a purple glow,

And evening full of the linnet's wings.

I will arise and go now, for always night and day

I hear lake water lapping with low sounds by the shore;

While I stand on the roadway, or on the pavements grey,

I hear it in the deep heart's core.

## Wendi: Of Good Books—The Power and the Fear

Some time ago a mother asked for help understanding why we might read a book like George MacDonald's *The Princess and the Goblin*.

The discussion reminded me of my experience with the sequel, *The Princess and Curdie*. I read it as a very young child—so young I don't remember how young, and for a very long time I couldn't remember the title of the book. In fact, over the years the details of the story slipped away to the point that my memory of most of that story was hidden in the mists of other memories, other books, other experiences. Then one day when I was in my very late twenties, busy with my life in Japan as a young military wife and mom, the memory of that book came out of the mists, recalled by a stray reference.

I was reading one of those special children's book catalogs that used to abound—catalogs as literary as the books inside them, chatty, personable. The catalog writer explained that she had read this book as a child and over the years had forgotten all but a single detail of the story—something about a grandmother with a fire of rose petals that never lost their rose petal essence (similar to the burning bush in the Bible), and you could put your hand in it without harm. She found this detail in *The Princess and Curdie* while reviewing it for the catalog. With a thrill she recognized her old friend and was delighted, and it all came flooding back.

That fire of rose petals is the one detail I also had remembered, so I too was thrilled to find my old friend again. I promptly added the title to the others on my order form and sent it off (snail mail, as one did in those days). I was even more delighted when the book arrived several weeks later and I read it again as an adult. The sequel is just that good, and the first book is even better.

MacDonald was a devout Christian and a pastor devoted to his flock—and his God. His books are somewhat allegorical. For some reason, there are people who don't care for them (I don't understand it); but I would not recommend avoiding them based on secondhand opinion. At least skim through them yourself before making your decision.

It is true that not every book is every person's cup of tea (and children are born persons). But it isn't true that merely not liking a book is a sound reason to avoid it. Nor is it good policy to avoid books merely because they have scary things like planned goblin invasions, greedy trolls, and dark caverns in them. A book that frightens one child encourages another. A book that makes no impression on one child will be a never-to-be-forgotten source of courage for another.

We cannot know in advance what a book will be to our children. We often think we know, but my own children surprised me again and again. I also have now heard hundreds of times from mothers who say they were sure their child would loathe or be bored by this book or another, only to discover it was the newest favourite. Children, like the rest of us, are people of many parts, and we should give them the dignity of being complex human beings with depths we have not yet plumbed and may never.

Children have many different reactions to different stories—some good, some bad. I knew a child afraid of beavers after being frightened by talking beavers in *The Lion, The Witch and the Wardrobe*. I would not avoid a book widely recognized as a well-written children's classic merely because another child was afraid of the dark after reading it. Consider the fact that it is recognized as a well-written classic. While that is not alone a stamp of approval and compatibility with your belief system, it does indicate that thousands more children (and their parents) have been blessed and have grown in their understanding because of it. Their experience should be weighed in our decisions as well if the reactions of other children is our measurement.

We can also use such knowledge to help with a book rather than to reject it. If reading a book makes one child afraid of the dark or another afraid of rats or granddaddy longlegs or whatever, use that knowledge to help that young reader work through it and deal with it. Real life is not sugar-coated and lined with cotton wool. Children will come face to face with terrors of their own, both real and imagined. It is better to deal with those first in a fictional story between the pages of a book that can be put down. Real life is full of choices of right and wrong, bravery and cowardice, and people who make the wrong choice. Real books give children some exposure and practice in considering those choices, thinking about the implications, imagining what they would do in similar circumstances.

Well-written books come alive in our minds. They bring us into the scene. These powerful descriptions, scene setting, and skillful building of worlds feed our imaginations, warm them, bring them to life, and give the reader an excellent exposure to the skill of writing and the power of words. While we don't want to inundate children with frights and horrors or to ignore sensitivities and maturity levels altogether, we also don't want to avoid all possible ways they might become afraid, all misdeeds, or all wrong choices. We all have and have had fears for good reasons and for ignoble reasons and for silly reasons. It's a blessing to be able to recognize them for what they are and have help facing them when young in safe circumstances rather than regarding them as something to avoid at all costs. MacDonald's story of Curdie, the goblins, and the princess is really lovely and living and deserves to be judged on its own merits, not on secondhand information (not even mine). Please let your understanding of this book—and every other book—be based primarily on your own reading, not just on what a few negative witnesses have claimed.

(*2018 post from* Archipelago)

## Lynn: The Virtues of Tea

A pot of tea can change your children's lives. It did mine one day!

On that fall Friday afternoon, with lessons finished and the children happily creating a parallel universe of some sort in the backyard, I brewed myself a little pot of Earl Grey and settled into an oomphy chair to revel in a moment of satisfaction over what I appraised as a well-rounded week of lessons—the rarest of rarities! But then, through the steam rising from my cup, my eyes happened upon a stack of oh-so-thoughtfully chosen poetry and art books gathering dust in a corner. Ohhh, I thought, then there's *that*...

Feeling less smug, I rued the many weeks that slip past with no time to squeeze in these disciplines of beauty. Days are consumed with managing the flow of routines and getting necessary facts into little heads like stuffing kindling into a firebox. But what use is dry kindling without lighting and stoking a fire? I sighed over unexplored poems, art, symphonies, Psalms, even family folklore—those inspirations that spark the kindling in our heads and draw fire and light into the furnace of the heart.

I knew the dust would just gather deeper unless I found the missing habit, the pleasant ritual, that would weave the loose ends of these "disciplines of beauty" into the fabric of our days. I gazed into my cup of tea, growing cooler by the minute.

Suddenly resolved to minimize my margin for motherly regrets, I dusted off a poetry book, fetched more teacups, and called in the children. And though I did not realize it 'til many pots of tea later, in that one resolute motion the countenance of our afternoons was forever lightened. By some felicity of momentary grace, I just stumbled upon that pleasant ritual to steadily stoke those fires... daily teatime!

Around 3:30 p.m. or so, I simply stop whatever I'm doing—regardless of how much laundry is undone or whether school is finished or whether I have a clue about dinner—and enliven the air with some Bach or Handel or whomever we're thinking about at the time and put the kettle on. When the whistle blows, the children know by now to wrap up whatever they're doing and come set the table. Tea is steeping!

Our poetry books now have a handier home in my kitchen hutch, right below my teapot shelf. When tea is served, I read some poems—just a few, and we may talk about them or not. Sometimes we read silly poems, sometimes classics, some old, some new. Other times we look at an art book. Some days we read a Psalm. I keep it as short as the day calls for. Then we just linger for as long as the children care to visit. This little moment of ceremony has transformed us more than anything I can think of. It's what my children will remember long after the rest of it has fuzzed to a blur.

Now, before you protest that this sort of thing is beyond the realm of your reality, please understand: this is not an element of some sort of dream life. It often occurs amid piles of dirty dishes and unfolded laundry, atop a kitchen floor that, swept, would yield a hearty contribution to the compost! But I have confidence that the Lord will honor the good intentions of a mother's heart and somehow redeem this time for me in my busy life. "For thus saith the Lord God, the Holy One of Israel; In returning and rest shall ye be saved; in quietness and in confidence shall be your strength" (Isaiah 30:15).

True to that promise, teatime has brought forth much fruit. I have found that lots of narration bubbles forth during this time as the children recount for me all sorts of things they have read or done in their free time, usually without my bidding. Recently, I overheard one child reciting a verse while playing, and I asked her where she learned it. "From you, Mommy, at teatime!" she replied. I didn't even recall reading it, but it had impressed itself upon her! My children have begun voluntarily writing poetry as a result of our teatime readings too and are compiling them into little collections for binding. This is effortless fruit—the kind that reminds us that learning can be an easy yoke and joyful!

Keeping tea has other virtues for mothers as well. In the absence of the hustle and bustle of the dinner hour, we can more quietly train the habits, as Charlotte Mason would say—more steadily teach little nuances of mannerliness and how to handle fine things with care. Maybe the English and the Chinese have known this for centuries, but handling fine things automatically quiets the temperament. A child in a wild mood will come to a teacup and calm down just at the prospect of lifting it. I bought each of the children their own special china cup and saucer and presented them all wrapped up with great fanfare. It took only one broken teacup to impress upon the children to handle china gingerly; my daughter's heart was more broken than her cup when she saw it shatter all over the floor.

Everyone is more careful since then, and I had already resigned myself to losing a cup or two in the course of training—it's a small price to pay in the end for the vast improvement I see in their table manners. Teatime produces teachable moments to train habits of helping with kitchen tasks too. The children help me set out a little fruit, perhaps cheese and crackers or crunchy veggies, sometimes a few cookies, and always lemon, honey and milk, napkins and spoons... the works, and all in an orderly way.

Teatime offers lessons in cleanup cooperation as well. Dinner dishes, especially in a large family, multiply into daunting and discouraging proportions for training purposes. But learning to tidy up a few dishes from tea makes the task manageable for beginners. Teatime has also impressed upon my children the joy of serving. When we read *Felicity Learns a Lesson* (from the American Girl series), we came upon a dandy lesson in teatime etiquette. Felicity, a colonial girl, takes a finishing course wherein she is taught the art of taking and serving tea. All of it is spelled out in the book; I had nothing to teach! This inspired them to learn to serve others, the fruit of which is manifest across other situations as well. They are more mindful of being gracious, as both hostess and guest, for having this experience. Learning to serve others can be a pleasant lesson!

While I'm recounting the virtues of tea, here's another: with a little snack under our belts midafternoon, we avoid the sinking blood sugar crankies that used to greet Daddy when he came in the door every evening. Now we get through evening dinner preparations with a bit more cheer, and that means a lot to the man of the house! And, because of teatime, I have more control over snacks—with a healthy repast anticipated midafternoon, our junk food intake is well on the wane. It occurs to me that this daily habit of taking a moment away for renewal is in harmony with our creation, for how does our Father teach us, from the very beginning of things, to glorify Him? Through observing a time of rest. So it comes as no surprise that He slips into our tea conversation so often and that we come away from the table with restored and quiet hearts, in a better frame to serve the Lord and enjoy Him forever. Afternoon tea, that forgotten tonic of my wise English forbears, has become the golden hour of our days. Even when we travel, the children always remind me to pack the tea because they have come to covet the anchor of this quiet time apart with me! And wherever we take our tea habit, we invite others to join the fun, which has brought forth many broadening afternoons . . . like the teatime that prompted my grandmother to tell us tales of kinfolk she'd known who lived through the Civil War.

Some days, the rewards of my insistence are even sweeter. The children will come peacefully to me when teatime's done and the poetry and art books are closed—tummies full of warm tea and yummies, and heads full of beautiful symphonies, great words or fine pictures—and give me a long, quiet hug. I just sit and hold them until they let go, which is sometimes a surprisingly long time.

Ah, it's time for tea already! Good. Go on now, put your kettle on too!

> *"Bread and water can so easily be toast and tea."* (*Author Unknown*)

(*Lynn wrote this essay in 1998, and it is a cherished part of our website.*)

# A Conversation: Mostly about Food

**Lynn (Winter 2022):**

Temps are dropping here! Sure wish I could make y'all some chicken noodle soup and grilled pimiento cheese sandwiches (with garlic dill pickles on the side, of course). And a pot of tea. With double chocolate banana bread. We could all use some comfort food.

**Anne:**

I would absolutely be up for pimiento cheese right now. It's snowy and slippery and miserable out. Enjoy every one of those sandwiches, and the banana bread as well. (I hope that's not hypothetical.)

**Lynn:**

Here is the recipe. [Double Chocolate Banana Bread on the Smitten Kitchen website.] Stuff is no joke. I have been making it a bit too much, but it's so easy and magical, actually improves on the second day, and makes all my people adore me. LOL

I'll go ahead and say it: You're welcome.

**Donna-Jean:**

That looks fairly amazing.

**Lynn (a week later):**

Anne, is [what you made] the Double Chocolate Banana Bread from Smitten Kitchen?

**Anne:**

Yep. We only had two bananas, but it worked fine. [*And we have been making it ever since. Thank you, Lynn.*]

## Wendi: Sing Together

I was deeply blessed and encouraged at our camp in Tennessee this past summer when a lovely Brazilian mother living in America told me that singing the native folk music of her home country had been a beautiful, rich way for her kids to connect with their grandparents back home and to improve their accents and vocabulary at the same time. Singing folk songs connects generations, she told me, and it gave me goosebumps of delight to think about it—it really did, right then and there. Singing folk songs connects generations.

Sing. Sing together. Sing the happy songs, the sad songs, the tragic songs, the silly songs, the work songs, the love songs, the ballads, and the nonsensical songs. Sing.

In my opinion, the primary principle for folk songs in a Charlotte Mason education is just that: sing them. Sing them. This is about participatory, active, personal involvement, not a consumer or spectator activity. It doesn't matter if you don't like how you sound. Sing anyway. It doesn't matter if you've never done this before. Sing anyway. There are sound physiological reasons for this—singing increases happy hormones, reduces stress, regulates your breathing. Research shows that singing together is an activity that improves bonding, strengthens relationships, and just makes people feel more connected to each other—and couldn't we all use more of that in a family? It doesn't take more time; it saves you time. By taking time to sing fun folk songs together, you not only get the benefits that come from the act of singing, but you also lighten your day. Increasing the sense of cooperative, unified spirit, as folk singing does, will repay you by making the rest of your day go more smoothly.

Hymns also do this, but hymns are not usually pitched in the easy, suitable-for-children way that folk songs are. They aren't about silly situations, and they don't have the seemingly meaningless but rhythmic folderol refrains that give children mouth music and play with sounds and syllables and rhyme scheme. You can play around with folk songs—singing them together as you do chores, go on road trips, sit in the dark during a power outage—playfully messing about with the lyrics to make them funny, to make them match what you are doing or things that are happening in your lives in ways that might feel irreverent should you try them with hymns.

I know I've said all this before, but we also have new families who are hearing this for the first time.

Please, give them a fair trial if you haven't already and sing folk songs together.

(*2019 post from* Archipelago, *written shortly after our AO Camp Meeting*)

## Anne: The Naming of Clouds

Our family spent a lot of years living in a house with a big ground-level window in the basement. I always loved watching the robins, grackles, and Northern Flickers that would come right up to the glass, digging for food or just hanging out. Our window looked out from the room where we usually did school, so the girls got used to Mom's bird-sighting interruptions. ("Quick, get the book!")

Later, when we were down to one teenager living at home, we moved to a fifteenth-floor apartment, where we got some flybys but not many drop-ins; so I switched my out-the-window interest to clouds. Clouds are universal and free to everyone. You can watch clouds in the city, the country, or the suburbs; you don't have to pay admission at a cloud park, and you can't create clutter by collecting them. But after a while, like birds or anything else, you realize it's not enough just to look: it's time to find out more.

So I found a book by Richard Hamblyn called *The Invention of Clouds: How an Amateur Meteorologist Forged the Language of the Skies*. It tells how Luke Howard settled on the system of cloud names that he did, why that has lasted over two hundred years, and how that fits in with a bigger idea: that simple principles, simply stated, are often the best.

Since ancient times, natural philosophers and poets had tried to come up with words for kinds of clouds, and sailors and farmers had created their own nicknames, like "mares' tails." By the nineteenth century, scientists wanted to classify and organize everything they could see—animals, plants, fossils—and give them names. Then when they went exploring and found a new species of fern, they would know exactly where it fit into the hierarchy of ferns. But the fact that clouds never stayed the same for long, their *mutability*, was something that eluded classification for years.

Luke Howard was a Quaker pharmacist who studied weather in his spare time. In 1802 when Howard was about thirty years old, he presented his "Essay on the Modification of Clouds" to a small group of scientists called the Askesian Society, and his findings were then published in a scientific journal. Richard Hamblyn's book, summarizing Howard's essay, says clouds have:

> shapes and forms due to physical processes that affect water present in the atmosphere...and although unexpected complexities and complications arise due to the instability of the circulating atmosphere, the physical principles of cloud formation are as easily understood as any other natural process. (p. 120)

But how could the shapes and forms be classified? A workable system for naming clouds needed to have not too many categories or descriptive terms, but not too few either; and it had to be expressed in clear, objective language. Howard chose to use the international language of classification, Latin, to name three main categories or, as he called them, modifications of clouds—*cumulus* (the fluffy ones), *stratus* (the ones like a layer or a blanket), and *cirrus* (the light, wispy ones). Since clouds were all about change and movement, he added four other terms for combined and transitional clouds like *cirrostratus* and *cirrocumulus*. But this was not just a list of vocabulary words; by naming the forms, Howard was also shaping our understanding of the objects themselves.

Quite soon after Luke Howard created his names for clouds, the criticism and the "I can do it better" started. One common criticism was elitism because he had used fancy, unfamiliar Latin terms. At the same time, a man named John Bostock said that Howard's system was "much too confined to be of any great use" (Hamblyn,

p. 149), so in other words, it wasn't complicated enough to be scientific.

In a letter to a scientific journal, Bostock suggested a whole different way of categorizing clouds, but not in Latin, using terms such as an "arc," a "linear arc," a "mottled arc," a "wreathed arc," and so on. He also suggested such highly scientific words as "Tufts," which were "clouds which resemble bunches of hair, the fibres of which are sometimes disposed in a perfectly irregular manner"; and "Flocks," which, he said, are "when clouds form larger and [more] compact masses than those which I have called 'tufts'" (Hamblyn, p. 150). Howard published a rebuttal of Bostock's system, and Bostock wrote back saying that he wasn't really trying to say that his terms were better than Howard's. However, since that was pretty much what he actually was saying, nobody took him too seriously after that.

Next, one of Howard's own friends and supporters, Thomas Forster, tried to add a number of extra Latin terms to the list. When that didn't go over well, he suggested a kinder, simpler, more Anglo-Saxon-sounding set of words, such as "curl-cloud," "stacken-cloud," and "fall-cloud." Some scientists gave those words a try, but they eventually dropped them as well in favour of *cirrus*, *cumulus*, and *stratus*—terms that then became familiar to farmers and sailors and anyone else in the world who wanted to record and study weather patterns. Every attempt to come up with something better failed because Howard's system had *clarity*.

Just as Luke Howard created a language to describe clouds, Charlotte Mason created what she first called a synopsis to communicate the key principles, the vital ideas of lifelong learning. These educational principles work for many of the same reasons as Howard's cloud principles. They are timeless; they describe what we need to know in just enough detail; and they can be applied in many contexts, times, and places. They are based on simple truths about what human beings are like, what we want, and how we learn. Charlotte Mason said that some of what she proposed might seem too easy but that of course it was "easy and natural" (*Home Education*, p. 10) because it matched up with what was there—in the same way that Howard's descriptions matched actual clouds. She described aspects of learning that had been recognized for centuries, but she combined them with new discoveries in areas such as neuroscience, which are now being confirmed and expanded on by breakthroughs from our own era.

But right there you might be wondering: If we know now that our brains are much more complex than we ever dreamed, haven't we outgrown the simple terms of earlier times? Absolutely not. The point is that it has taken some of our most brilliant minds to explore huge, complex ideas and state them in essential terms. Children are born persons. $E = mc^2$. The theory of everything. God so loved the world.

Recently I read the book *Essentialism* by Greg McKeown. McKeown describes essentialism as having a singleness and clarity of purpose, discerning what really matters. Rather than just thinking "less," it's really "more"—more of what matters to us. This kind of essentialism is not a decorating aesthetic; it makes room for beauty and understands about laundry. When we find joy in the educational path we've chosen, we no longer have to make excuses for not taking up the latest homeschool fad, reading the latest book, or signing up for another activity. On the other hand, we can feel free to use tools from many sources, to draw on scientists and commentators and poets and our own life experiences, to make unexpected connections and build unusual relationships. Essentialism is recognizing that we have the power to choose what matches or works with the picture we're creating and to let the rest go. When we have a focus, a priority, or as Charlotte Mason said, a King to serve, the choices we make fall into place.

## The Truth Is There to Be Discovered

Here are some other similarities I noticed between Luke Howard's system and Charlotte Mason's principles. First, they didn't appear magically. Charlotte Mason didn't even want to take credit for "inventing" the PNEU principles; she felt that they already existed, like gravity, and she was just there like Sir Isaac Newton to point them out. How did Luke Howard seem to see clouds so clearly? He did everything he could to put himself at the center of their study. He went to meetings of the Askesian Society; he talked to other scientists; he read the thoughts of the past as well as the most up-to-date journals. He spent time observing clouds from an upstairs room in his house in the country; I think he might have enjoyed our fifteenth-floor view. He used his regular commuting journey to study the sky. He even travelled to the Lake District, where Charlotte Mason would live years later, on a walking tour with his business partner and fellow science enthusiast William Allen. Hamblyn's book says that Howard made "watercolour sketches of the clouds as they formed over the mountains of the Lakes" (p. 176). He says the two men "rose early to go hill walking, climbing some of the loftiest mountains in order to enjoy the views; they took picnics upon the summits, and tracked the changes of atmospheric pressure with their portable barometers" (p. 173). Howard wrote himself about their climb up Helvellyn, which is the third-highest place in England, that they saw "a fine and truly gratifying view to a meteorologist of large cumuli mixing with the mountains, gliding up the valleys and sailing by us with their round summits beneath our feet while the [higher storm clouds]...poured down rain upon our heads" (Hamblyn, p. 173). He said that it was amazing to finally be so close to the clouds he had been studying for so long, even if he got wet.

Charlotte Mason also put herself at the center of working and living out her philosophy. She surrounded herself with something like Luke Howard's science group and his close friends, only in her case it was the Parents' National Educational Union and her own set of kindred spirits. She read about old and new theories of education. She observed the children of the House of Education school, and she read letters and examination papers from hundreds of families and schools who were using the methods. She helped organize large meetups and conferences. And she ran into criticism and argument even while the list of principles was being formulated—even from some of her own people, who left the PNEU over those disagreements. Still, she held onto the methods she believed were true and to the terms that held the most *clarity*.

Mason's principles were not based on self-interest—for herself, or for us. She said that a due ordering of the process of education would "awaken and direct mind hunger so that everyone's mind will look after itself" (*A Philosophy of Education*, p. 281), but she didn't intend that to mean so that everyone's mind will look after itself *for itself*. This isn't about self-help; this is about serviceability, being available to others, having an outward focus. Mason felt that she was a steward over the principles of education; but, like Luke Howard, she knew how to defend them when she had to, even if it meant risking personal relationships.

## Learning Is Change, Change Is Learning

A second similarity between Howard's principles and Mason's is that both systems acknowledged the importance of change. Hamblyn says that "Howard's breakthrough was breathtaking because it granted the clouds their mobility instead of willing them to be still for the benefit of science" (p. 124). Children's minds do not stay still for the benefit of our lesson plans; they are growing and changing, and therefore our family dynamics and school needs change too.

In adult education, there is a theory of transformational learning, which is that what we learn in a transformative or personal context changes who we are. Critics point out that there is really no other kind of learning—that every connection we make changes our physiological brains. Mason said that we have possibilities for good and for evil but that we are liberated by understanding our potential for change. Nothing we get by nature or nurture has to be permanently stuck to us; or, as she puts it, "the educability of children is enormously greater than has hitherto been supposed, and is but little dependent on such circumstances as heredity and environment" (*A Philosophy of Education*, pp. xxx–xxxi). This is not a boastful or a heretical concept; when we see that this is the way God created us and the Spirit works in us, then we can work with that instead of against it. (When I posted a photo of clouds online, someone commented, "I love clouds, and I love what wind does to clouds." That's it exactly!)

And change needs to lead to action. The final section of McKeown's *Essentialism* is "Execute." The Bible and the ancient philosophers said the same thing: what you do comes out of who you are, but if you don't act on it, then you aren't.

## Natural Boundaries

A third similarity is the recognition of limits or boundaries. In Charlotte Mason's fourth principle, for example, she says that, for teachers and parents:

> These principles are limited by the respect due to the personality of children, which must not be encroached upon whether by the direct use of fear or love, suggestion or influence, or by undue play upon any one natural desire. (*A Philosophy of Education*, p. xxix)

There are certain methods of teaching that are good and some that are okay, but there are others that may be effective but are morally offensive and off-limits.

A more general example of limits that has been popular in recent years is living with a smaller wardrobe. Greg McKeown actually uses the clothes-closet idea throughout his book as an illustration of making choices: recognizing limits and saying that "enough" does not apply only to how many pairs of shoes you allow into your closet but, more generally, what ideas you allow into your mind, especially with all that information flying by through social media. Some of it is good, but it might not be your good right now—just like wearing three-inch heels might be your good, but it's not mine. Essentialism celebrates not what we're missing out on but the abundance of what we have and our power to choose.

Charlotte Mason's principle 19 is that "children should be taught, as they become mature enough to understand such teaching, that the chief responsibility which rests on them as persons is the acceptance or rejection of ideas" (*A Philosophy of Education*, p. xxxi). This is why we require students to narrate instead of filling in worksheets. They might leave gaps in a narration, but that's part of storytelling. This is also why Laurie Bestvater's book *The Living Page* was groundbreaking; she pointed out that in any kind of notebook, just as on any bookshelf or in any shoe closet, there is only so much space. Our inclination is to squeeze in as much as we can because we don't like gaps. We worry about gaps, especially in schoolwork; we are afraid that somebody is going to call us out on the fact that we left out something important. But the point of, say, a Book of Centuries, as Bestvater points out, is to help us stick to the original, simple idea rather than packing everything we can find into a hernia-producing, unabridged world history index. Think of it as a backpack instead of a giant suitcase.

Now, focusing on a simple idea does not mean your life will be simple. Some people have multiple plates they're spinning, but they're all important; some just have one or two right now, but that could change. The bigger problem for many people is dealing with the places where they have said yes but should be saying no. They are struggling with expectations and assumptions that are making things harder, not simpler; or they are taking on responsibilities that belong to others, including their children. Charlotte Mason said that we all need to develop our own character muscles to use the will and that if we try to take over other people's opportunity to do that, we're taking what belongs to them. Saying "You figure that one out" is an essentialist *and* a Charlotte Mason attitude. (Does that make you feel better?)

## Balancing the Particular with the General

A fourth similarity is the balance between the particular and the general, the uniqueness of "children are born persons," and the universality of "education is the science of relations." Luke Howard saw that clouds have "many individual shapes but few basic forms" (Hamblyn, p. 120). He was awed by the uniqueness of each cloud, but he was also able to define what made it a cloud—in relationship with other clouds and with ice, snow, and wind. We need to choose the unique elements that respect our differences as families and individuals but also explore the ideas that are universal. Minimalist writers have pointed out that you shouldn't become a minimalist for the sake of minimalism; in the same way, you don't educate with Charlotte Mason's philosophy because your goal is to be a C.M. educator. The principles are like direction markers, but they are not the path itself or the destination. They are there to help you recognize essential truths and to allow you to get rid of the superficial, the clutter, the unhelpful sidebars so that you can focus on the children you're fostering, the goats you're breeding, the tomatoes you're canning, the glass you're blowing, the notebook you're filling, the missionaries and other quiet heroes you're supporting, the hearts you're encouraging, the clouds you're watching.

## First Held with Mental Grasp

Luke Howard's first essay on clouds was quickly translated into French and then into German. The German translator tried, as the English had, to find new words for Howard's Latin terms, but the best he could do was the German equivalent of "hair-clouds" and "heap-clouds." According to Hamblyn's book, he gave up on that altogether when he got to *cirro-stratus* and used the Latin words for all the types. The interesting part is that the famous poet Goethe agreed that patriotism and pride in language should stand aside for the sake of *clarity*.

About five years after this, Luke Howard received a letter from Goethe's secretary, saying that Goethe had written some verses in honour of "the man who distinguished cloud from cloud" (Hamblyn, p. 217) and that he was curious to know more about him. At first Howard thought that the letter was a prank, but it turned out that Goethe was very interested in shapes and patterns, such as snowflakes and clouds, and he became one of Howard's biggest promoters. The verses he wrote, translated into English, include these lines:

> But Howard gives us with his clear mind
> The gain of lessons new to all mankind;
> That which no hand can reach, no hand can clasp
> He first has gained, first held with mental grasp.
> (Hamblyn, p. 213)

Perhaps because we can't clasp clouds with our own hands, we can value all the more the clear vision that allowed Luke Howard to document their characteristics—especially when we then look up, from whatever floor we live on, and see for ourselves how what he discovered about them is still true. We continue to learn from many writers and educators, past and present; but we find ourselves, more and more, returning to our worn pink paperbacks (or our nice new editions) containing Charlotte Mason's simple expression of a large idea, the twenty educational principles. So it seems most appropriate to end with the quote from Benjamin Whichcote that she used to introduce them: "No sooner doth the truth...come into the soul's sight, but the soul knows her to be her first and old acquaintance" (*A Philosophy of Education*, p. xxix).

(*A talk given at the AO Camp Meeting in 2019*)

# Only by Prayer

Spiritual teaching, like the wafted odour of flowers, should depend on which way the wind blows. Every now and then there occurs a holy moment, felt to be holy by mother and child, when the two are together—that is the moment for some deeply felt and softly spoken word about God, such as the occasion gives rise to. Few words need be said, no exhortation at all; just the flash of conviction from the soul of the mother to the soul of the child. Is "Our Father" the thought thus laid upon the child's soul? There will be, perhaps, no more than a sympathetic meeting of eyes hereafter, between mother and child, over a thousand showings forth of "Our Father's" love; but the idea is growing, becoming part of the child's spiritual life. This is all: no routine of spiritual teaching; a dread of many words, which are apt to smother the fire of the sacred life; much self-restraint shown in the allowing of seeming opportunities to pass; and all the time, earnest purpose of heart, and a definite scheme for the building up of the child in the faith. It need not be added that, to make another use of our Lord's words, "this kind cometh forth only by prayer." It is as the mother gets wisdom liberally from above, that she will be enabled for this divine task. (*Home Education*, p. 348)

## Leslie: How Calvary Chapel Helped Shape AO

You may not know who Chuck Smith is. But if you use AmblesideOnline—even if you use only AO's artist or composer rotation, you have directly benefited from his ministry.

The AO Advisory represents various Christian faiths: Baptist, Lutheran, Church of Christ, Primitive Baptist, and Mennonite Brethren, with all of their rich traditions of hymn singing and old-fashioned preaching. And then there's me, with my non-denominational Calvary Chapel contemporary praise and worship. I have been influenced by the Calvary Chapel movement for my entire Christian life, and I see some definite parallels between AO and Calvary Chapel. AO has the same top-down leadership model, with the Advisory making decisions: we seek to be true to our vision rather than appealing to the changing whims of a user base.

I don't often like to pull out the "AO was my idea" card because, although the initial curriculum concept was mine, the creation of the booklist was mostly the work of the more well-read members of the Advisory. My fantastic brilliance was not in putting together a curriculum but in putting together the right people, persuading them that the project wasn't such a crazy idea, and then convincing them that it was something doable. Then I mostly stepped back and relegated myself to the role of webmaster. But I'm pulling out that card now. AO was my idea. And perhaps my biggest contribution, aside from recognizing who needed to be involved, was the insistence from its inception that it needed to be something that anybody, anywhere could use for free. Nobody should ever have to pay us, or me, to utilize AmblesideOnline. AO was (and is) run by volunteers who view the project as a ministry. That is Calvary

Chapel's influence, modeled after Pastor Chuck Smith's emphasis on blessing others as a ministry, not a profit venture, even though we, the AO Advisory, recognize the obvious marketing potential of AmblesideOnline.

This is a more personal look at my own history and my own life, which has been largely influenced and inspired by Chuck Smith and Calvary Chapel. I became a Christian in 1983 while in the military in Okinawa. The group of young Christians I fell in with talked in glowing terms about this church called Calvary Chapel back in California that welcomed young people and taught straight out of the Bible. So when I ended up stationed in Oceanside, California, I naturally looked them up. The first time I walked into a Calvary Chapel (I think it was a midweek Bible study), there was a guy up front with an acoustic guitar and a girl sitting on a stool next to him singing and leading worship. It seemed natural, no hype, and very real. It felt like coming home. The teaching was plain—no yelling, no theatrics, just a guy talking, explaining the Bible in a way I could understand—and that was refreshing.

During the three years between military and marriage, I was a part of the congregation of Calvary Chapel Oceanside. (At the time, they were meeting at the local YMCA, and we would hear YMCA announcements from the concession stand over the PA during church service: "Number 4, your pizza is ready!") Every chance I got, I would go with friends to "Big Calvary," which is what we called Chuck Smith's church in Costa Mesa, about an hour away. Often that was their Friday night Christian concerts. We were also going to Thursday night Bible studies at Calvary Chapel Dana Point, where Chuck Smith, Jr. was teaching; and I went to a women's Bible study at Calvary Chapel Vista taught by Cheryl Broderson, Chuck Smith's daughter. Being young and single and a brand-new Christian, I spent a lot of my spare time listening to sermons on cassette—mostly Chuck Smith. And when Calvary Chapel started a radio station (KWVE), I listened to a lot of Calvary Chapel teaching: Greg Laurie, Raul Ries, Jon Courson,

Don Johnson. Thus, much of my understanding of what it means to live as a Christian was learned from Calvary Chapel—either directly from Pastor Chuck or indirectly from one of his students who had gone on to plant a church somewhere else.

During that time, I met a recently divorced guy at work who was interested in Christianity, so I directed him to the one Christian I knew at work, who was involved in a spin-off Calvary Chapel church called Horizon Christian Fellowship, pastored by Mike Macintosh. The guy ended up becoming a Christian, and a year or so later, I married him.

We went to Horizon Christian Fellowship and Maranatha Chapel, another Calvary Chapel spin-off where Ray Bentley was the pastor. Horizon was meeting in an old school the county was no longer using. When the church needed a larger facility for Sunday morning services, they built a gymnasium at the church's expense on the school grounds that they could leave as a gift to the county when the county needed the school back. While the church was using the school grounds, they would allow kids from the neighborhood to use the gym when church services weren't going on. That generosity impressed me and modeled the ideal for me of how Christians should act toward their neighbors.

When my husband and I started our family a couple of years later, we decided we'd like our children to grow up in a more rural area where they could have a more normal childhood, away from the gang violence that was increasing in San Diego; so we drove from San Diego to Tennessee with a four-year-old and a two-year-old. During the very long drive, we listened to praise band cassettes from Maranatha Music, the music division of Calvary Chapel. We were confident we'd have no problem finding a church—after all, we were going to be living in the Bible Belt. But it wasn't as easy as we had expected. There were plenty of churches, but nothing with the kind of Bible teaching we had grown accustomed to. We even found a church that was sort of a copy of California mega-churches; I think it would be considered a "seeker church." They had rules they made new members read before joining—rules about what wasn't allowed (no hand-lifting, for example) because it might make new people uncomfortable. They did succeed in making anyone who walked in from the street comfortable, and the worship was similar to what we had known back in California, but the Bible teaching was not as doctrinally rich as we had been used to. We had hoped our dreams of finally finding a home church would be realized, but we were there for only two weeks.

One morning during our search for a church family, I woke up and it hit me—the natural, reverent, Spirit-seeking, Bible-teaching kind of church that I had taken for granted for the past ten years was something I had left back in California; I would never experience that again. It was gone forever. The realization hit me with force, and I wondered—what had we done? Had it been a mistake leaving California? At that point we began praying that a Calvary Chapel would be planted in our area, although the chances of that happening seemed remote. Eventually, though, it did happen after we met another family who had also moved from California and were praying for the same thing. We started our own little home Bible study, and that was the seed of the Calvary Chapel we were involved in for over twenty years. That church is still going strong, but we have moved from there and are currently involved with a Calvary Chapel that's a little closer.

Calvary Chapel isn't the perfect church. In fact, I've had my own issues with a few things, mostly when homeschooling has changed my perspective. As I learned about attachment parenting (Dr. Sears, the attachment parenting writer, used to do a call-in radio show on KWVE, so even my parenting style resulted from Calvary Chapel's influence), I wished the church were more family-inclusive instead of dividing worship, Bible studies, and church events into age groups, separating families into different rooms and activities. As I homeschooled (after hearing James Dobson talk about it, also on KWVE) and read more as a result, I couldn't find anyone there who had read or even valued classic literature. I noticed that there was frequent encouragement to be like Peter, the uneducated "fisher of men," but never like Moses or Paul, who were highly educated and wrote much of the Bible, leaving me with a sense that the church did not value more intellectual pursuits. This was not an official church-sanctioned attitude; more likely, it was an unintended consequence for this church whose focus was on saving souls via street evangelism and on recovery of drug addicts. In fact, many group leaders and even some pastors came from that background. So the church is not perfect, but no church is, and I've found that the positives far outweigh the negatives.

So we helped plant our local little Calvary Chapel and made that our church home. But any time I had to miss church because of a sick child, I'd tune in to Calvary Chapel's live service from Costa Mesa and listen to Pastor Chuck. In fact, the last time I was home with a sick child and tuned in happened to be the morning Pastor Chuck made the announcement that he had cancer. Maybe it wasn't just coincidence that I happened to stay home that morning, of all mornings—maybe I needed to prepare for the inevitable.

One Wednesday evening in fall 2013, we had a real treat—Terry Clark, a musician we had known of from Horizon Christian Fellowship in San Diego, gave a concert. At *our* little church in Tennessee! It was wonderful, heavenly, like a taste of home. During the music, I had the distinct feeling that there was a reason for the magical feeling of the worship—almost like a last victory celebration or a farewell. And I found out the very next morning that Pastor Chuck had died during the night, just a few hours after that concert.

Are you wondering what my church history has to do with AmblesideOnline? As I mulled over Pastor Chuck's death and my own years as a Christian that have been entirely under his shadow, I've realized how much of his teaching has influenced my own actions. I've also been struck by a couple of parallels. During the few months preceding his death, for the only time in the history of AO, I had seriously considered walking away from AO a couple of times. AO has had its (small) share of critics over the years, as any organization does. At that time, we had been alarmed to see our project reposted, renamed, even sold, so we had to become more diligent and responsible about protecting the work. As a result of our protection, I heard AO come under some pretty severe attack. Most of the attacks were variations of "AO is stingy" because even though we allow people to use it for free, we can't allow it to be copied, renamed, reposted, or sold. During those times that I was tempted to defend AO, I would hear Pastor Chuck's voice in the back of my mind as he answered a question once asked in an interview about how he responded to those who criticized him or his ministry. (You know that a person in the limelight as much as he was probably had all kinds of things said about him.) He said he refused to defend himself—that it was his job to continue doing what God had told him to do and it was God's job to defend him if that was necessary. I took that to heart. And, as far as me walking away from AO, I suddenly had the verses about "not being weary in doing good" (Galatians 6:9, NIV) and "since through God's mercy we have this ministry, we do not lose heart" (2 Corinthians 4:1, NIV) pop up at uncanny times frequently enough during that time to convince me that I was supposed to continue what I was doing, so walking away from AO was now off the table. That was no longer an option I entertained; to the current day, my commitment to AO is unwavering.

The other parallel is about the realities of all organizations. At the time we were praying for a Calvary Chapel to start in our rural area, we were told that the process of starting a Calvary Chapel wasn't as easy as the days I remembered back in California, when anyone could rent a storefront and hang a Calvary Chapel sign on the door. There had been a lot of problems with spin-off churches bearing the Calvary Chapel name but being doctrinally off, so "Big Calvary" had started to require that all Calvary Chapels must be under the official organization and meet certain doctrinal standards. When I see AO going through some of the same growing pains, it's encouraging to know that even an organization as spirit-filled and well-intentioned as Calvary Chapel has had similar growing pains, though on a much larger scale. They felt justified in protecting their vision and upholding standards of those who wanted to join them, so it's not wrong for AO to do the same thing.

Calvary Chapel has lost their earthly leader—the one who drove, inspired, and directed them—and I'm curious to know what that will mean for them. Similarly, in 1923, Charlotte Mason died, leaving her project without the one who drove, inspired, and directed it. Mrs. Steinthal, Mrs. Franklin, and all those others whose names I know from *Parents' Review* articles carried on the work for her successfully. Yet it wasn't the same. Without her wise but warm presence, listening and guiding with a smile but never any word that "left the least sting" (*In Memoriam*, p. 95), it couldn't be the same. Times were changing; the needs of the school system were putting pressure on the PNEU to make changes. Without Charlotte Mason there to hold firmly to the original vision, I'm sure things were done that she would never have wanted, compromises made to meet the demands of modern educational board requirements. AO tries to model what a C.M. education would look like if C.M. were alive today, but we can't know for sure what concessions she might have made to accommodate today's society. Would she ban the use of computers for her students? Would she encourage BBC productions of *Pride and Prejudice* or *Our Mutual Friend*? Even if one of the Steinthals or Franklins or others of her students were here to ask, they aren't Charlotte Mason, and they'd only be making an educated guess.

I tuned in to the live broadcast of the Sunday service at Calvary Chapel of Costa Mesa when I originally typed this. During the service, Chuck Smith's son told a few anecdotes about him and said that Pastor Chuck loved nature and knew the names of the birds and trees in his local area. I like to think that maybe he and Charlotte Mason are taking nature walks in heaven together. There's a glorious thought!

(*2013 post from* Archipelago)

## Wendi: Why Sing Hymns?

My eldest daughter and her husband have been singing with their kids forever. Okay, not literally forever, as her kids are not very old: five, four, three, and one. However, from the children's perspective it is forever because she was singing hymns to them when they were still in the womb. I have a vivid memory of her singing to her firstborn while he was being resuscitated after being born gray, limp, and unresponsive. I am positive he stayed with us to hear more of his mother's songs.

Very recently this busy family has been working specifically on the hymn "Trust and Obey." This mainly means they make sure to sing it every day in a more focused, intentional way. I could tell "Trust and Obey" was their current hymn because while the grandchildren were visiting me recently, they gathered themselves and their baby cousins together on my stairs and sang most of the hymn together. My grandma heart was warmed to the core. Imagine the joy of hearing your small grandchildren spontaneously singing hymns together just for fun, because they want to.

A couple of days ago, the four-year-old unfortunately did not obey. This resulted in an unplanned trip to the emergency room where she had to have a blood draw to determine just how dangerous her disobedience had been. To be honest, it was a pretty rough experience for them all, perhaps especially for our small granddaughter. Her brother was born with a medical condition requiring regular blood draws, so she knows more about it than most four-year-old children. When she saw the white-coated staff coming toward her, she knew what to expect, and she was upset.

Her mama offered to sing to her to help her think about something else and asked what song she would like Mommy to sing.

She was still thinking about what song she wanted when the process began. It wasn't their fault—the ER room was swamped, and other patients were waiting. The staff was as kind as possible, but they were forced to rush. They began with back-to-back simultaneous and brutal sticks—again, not their fault. She is not an easy stick. It was at the moment this torture began that my granddaughter blurted out her answer to her mama's question—she sobbed out "Trust and Obey!" as the hymn she needed her mommy to sing.

Paul and Silas sang hymns in prison, and they were able to do that because they already knew hymns and were used to singing them. She was able to come up with that hymn when she needed it because she already knew it. It's a recent part of her family stock of songs. She endured while Mommy sang. But more was yet to come. They took the finished blood draws and dashed out of the room so they could quickly get it to the lab and move on to other patients. Not much later a nurse returned, saying, "Bad news. One of them clotted before they could analyze it. I'm afraid we need another draw."

Can you imagine how my little granddaughter must have felt when she heard this? What do you suppose she was thinking when someone else came in and chatted gently with her while looking for another vein to jab in this petite morsel of a four-year-old?

Would you believe that she was thinking of another hymn to sing and even choosing the order? (She is a bit of a control freak at times.)

While the nurse was searching for her vein, my nervous and fearful granddaughter asked her Mama, "Can you sing 'Jesus Loves Me' and 'Trust and Obey?' Sing 'Jesus Loves Me' until she puts the needle in, and then sing 'Trust and Obey.'" She then started chatting with the nurse about this song her family listens to on the computer and then sings together at home and how it goes...and she sang a good chunk of "Trust and Obey" on her own to the nurse. My daughter tells me the nurse listened for a while and then said, "I just think it's so special that you sing with them like this!"

We are all very encouraged and inspired by this story, although the irony is not lost upon us that she had this opportunity to share this "testimony" with the nurse precisely because she had not obeyed. She is not a holier-than-thou, priggish miss who never does anything she shouldn't. She is much more like the little girl in the Longfellow poem—the one with the curl in the middle of her forehead. ("When she was good, she was very, very good, but when she was bad, she was horrid!")

There are many children, and adults too, who might find deep comfort and sustenance in singing these old hymns in times of trial (or in expressing joy). But they cannot because they have never learned these hymns. Some Christians don't really even see the point in learning hymns. It smacks of rote religion, I suppose, or perhaps it brings a faint whiff of fusty, musty, dead faith. I do not know why. I grew up in a family where a hymnal was a standard part of our things to do in the car on trips, and we sang hymns while doing dishes as naturally and easily as we argued over whose turn it was to do the dishes. It may be something "not done" anymore, but that doesn't mean it's outdated and old-fashioned. It means we are cut off from our roots.

> Is any among you happy?...merry?...sing praises...(James 5:13)

> I will sing with my spirit, but I will also sing with my mind. (1 Corinthians 14:15)

> ...Sing psalms, hymns, and spiritual songs with gratitude in your heart to God. (Colossians 3:16)

> Speak to one another with psalms, hymns, and spiritual songs. Sing and make music in your hearts to the Lord. (Ephesians 5:19)
>
> About midnight Paul and Silas were praying and singing hymns to God. (Acts 16:25)
>
> And when they had sung an hymn, they went out into the mount of Olives. (Matthew 26:30)
>
> (Verses are loosely paraphrased.)

Regular singing, both personal and congregational, of Psalms and hymns and spiritual songs has been part of the Christian tradition from the dawn of Christianity. It is the birthright of every child from a believing family. But we, like Esau, have squandered our heritage for a mess of pottage. Esau didn't want to bother to prepare or fetch his own food, and we don't think we need to sing our own songs any longer. In fact, we think we can't because we don't sound like trained musicians, so we might, at best, listen to somebody perform these songs once in a while. Listening to a performance may lift our spirits, but Christianity is not a spectator sport. It's personal. It's intimate. It's relationship.

We think the hymns that sustained the believers who went before us are too hard, too old-fashioned, out of date, irrelevant—especially to little children. My granddaughter is, of course, quite advanced for her years. She is bright beyond her chronology. Nevertheless, she is still only four years old. She was near panic in a very frightening and painful situation, yet even in that traumatized state, she was encouraged, strengthened, and comforted by a hymn over a hundred years old. In fact, it is the hymn that came to mind first for her. This happened because she knew the hymn, because her parents did not decide for her that she could not relate to it or understand it.

In a C.M. education we build relationships, develop good habits, and nurture affinities to complex ideas and practices such as singing hymns, personally engaging in observation for nature study, and enjoying poetry, art, and great books. We do these things when the children are young so that these connections are already there for them to draw on when they need them. While God can, of course, work miracles, most often He works with us where we are. Just the right hymn coming to mind when and where we need it is more likely to happen when those hymns are already a natural, integrated, whole part of our lives.

Please. Sing with your children.

P.S. Granddaughter's bloodwork all came back fine, and she left the ER saying to her mom, "I guess next time I should . . . obey."

(Thank you to my oldest daughter for many things: permission to share this story and edit your words for an AO publication, for being the mother you are to those precious children, and for choosing the good man you did to father those darlings. A big thank-you to all the mothers of my grandchildren because you all sing hymns with your children regularly and you all have married good men, so a story like this could have come from any of you.)

(*2016 post from* Archipelago, *written shortly after our conference in Texas*)

A map of the world must be a panorama to a child of pictures so entrancing that he would rather ponder them than go out to play; and nothing is more easy than to give him this *joie de vivre*. Let him see the world as we ourselves choose to see it when we travel; its cities and peoples, its mountains and rivers, and he will go away from his lesson with the piece of the world he has read about, be it county or country, sea or shore, as that of "a new room prepared for him, so much will he be magnified and delighted in it." All the world is in truth the child's possession, prepared for him, and if we keep him out of his rights by our technical, commercial, even historical, geography, any sort of geography, in fact, made to illustrate our theories, we are guilty of fraudulent practices. What he wants is the world and every bit, piece by piece, each bit a key to the rest. (*A Philosophy of Education*, p. 42)

# The Sun Never Sets on AO

*(Lynn Bruce, Lakeview Camp at Waxahachie, Texas, 2016)*

On a recent spring afternoon, we asked a question across all of AmblesideOnline's social media platforms: Facebook, Instagram, MeWe, and our forum. (Our forum now has nearly 25,000 subscribers.) It was a simple question:

Where are you?

There is a reason why we do not know. AmblesideOnline is free. It is also freely available. Anyone, anywhere can access any portion of our copyrighted curriculum without signing up, registering, or paying a fee. As a result, we have no way of knowing where this curriculum is currently being used.

Although we do not keep records of where AmblesideOnline students live, we know that the curriculum has found its way to homes around the globe. The Advisory and Auxiliary alone have had members living (at various times) in the United States, Canada, Poland, Ukraine, Australia, the Philippines, and Peru. At our 2016 conference in Texas, Lynn Bruce was so amazed by some of the stories we heard about people using the curriculum around the world that she said, "The sun never sets on AO!" And we think she was probably right.

And so we asked, "Where are you?" The answers to our question this spring were surprising and encouraging. Here is what our respondents told us:

- All 50 states of the United States of America, and the District of Columbia
- Canada, including Alberta, British Columbia, Manitoba, New Brunswick, Nova Scotia, Ontario, Prince Edward Island, Quebec, and Saskatchewan
- Australia, including all six states of New South Wales, Queensland, South Australia, Tasmania, Victoria, and Western Australia

Plus:

- Mexico
- Cuba
- El Salvador
- Guatemala
- Nicaragua
- Brazil
- Colombia
- Peru
- England
- Wales
- Ireland
- Northern Ireland
- Scotland
- France
- Germany
- Italy
- Kosovo
- Macedonia
- Netherlands
- Poland
- Portugal
- Spain
- Ukraine
- Turkey and Asia Minor
- Russia
- India
- Nepal
- China
- South Korea
- Japan
- Thailand
- Cambodia
- Malaysia
- Indonesia
- Timor-Leste
- Papua New Guinea
- Philippines
- New Zealand
- Vanuatu
- Marshall Islands
- United Arab Emirates
- "Middle East"
- Chad
- Ghana
- Kenya
- Niger
- Nigeria
- South Africa
- Tanzania
- Zambia
- Zimbabwe
- Military families
- And one who asked that we keep their location secret, due to their lack of freedom to tell us.

We pray for every family represented by these and other countries.

# Snippet 4

**Leslie:**

The past few weeks I've been sorting through my digital photos. Although I love looking through them, I'm mostly sad—sad because the tiny baby or the little child is gone forever. In the last part of *A Severe Mercy*, Sheldon Vanauken talks about time being a limitation of our human lives so that we can experience only one thing at a time. But his experience after losing his wife seemed to him to show that God (and our future heavenly bodies) exist outside of time and that we will experience people in their timeless form. Reliving his wife's life through her journals helped Vanauken form a unified sense of her essence (or soul) that was a composite of her at every age and stage, and that's how we'll experience one another once we live outside of time. He was able to form a perspective of the whole person—not the child and the teenager and the young wife as different forms of her but as a unified whole.

I don't totally understand it, but I think it means that the children I "lost" when they grew up aren't actually gone. Each age is still a part of the essence of the person; and when I meet them in heaven, they will have all of those things that I miss about them as children. No stage will have been lost; no age is gone forever. Somehow, this has the potential to be a comfort, though I haven't quite figured out how yet.

**Anne:**

What you have realized is what Lewis Carroll totally missed.

(*Emails, 2015*)

# Great Is Thy Faithfulness

*When we meet together in person, whether as an Advisory Board or to put on a conference for hundreds of others, we sing. We sang in an airport once; we sang around a campfire in Texas; we sang in a little bed and breakfast in Canada; we sang in Wendi's living room in Indiana; we sang at our own camp meeting in Tennessee—and so often we included the hymn that it became a theme for AmblesideOnline: "Great Is Thy Faithfulness."*

Great is Thy faithfulness,
O God my Father;
There is no shadow of turning with Thee;
Thou changest not, Thy compassions, they fail not;
As Thou hast been Thou forever wilt be.

*Refrain*

Great is Thy faithfulness!
Great is Thy faithfulness!
Morning by morning new mercies I see;
All I have needed Thy hand hath provided;
Great is Thy faithfulness, Lord, unto me!

Summer and winter, and springtime and harvest,
Sun, moon, and stars in their courses above
Join with all nature in manifold witness
To Thy great faithfulness, mercy, and love.

Pardon for sin and a peace that endureth,
Thine own dear presence to cheer and to guide;
Strength for today and bright hope for tomorrow,
Blessings all mine, with ten thousand beside!
(Thomas O. Chisholm)

# Karen: After a Gathering

It was a grand and glorious and blessed time— every single minute. Very rarely is so much joy and blessing pooled in one place, reflecting so much Light all at once.

Perhaps we could not bear it long, or often.

Or perhaps, in these frail bodies, we would do worse— grow inured to the heaven we are being allowed to see,

to take it for granted,

even to lose our taste for it.

So it comes but rarely,

to give us, for a moment only,

a glimpse of what heaven will be.

When we exist in a state which will be able to bear,

and celebrate

and worship

and glory

without growing weary or ceasing to appreciate it one iota the less.

(*Email, 2016*)

# Tribute to Wendi

In the summer of 2021, the AmblesideOnline Advisory members, including Wendi Capehart, were hard at work on a multivolume poetry project. We planned to include biographical sketches of several poets, but Wendi suddenly decided that two of the volumes needed biographical notes at the end; so she went ahead and wrote them because that's what Wendi did. She also contributed several of the sketches.

But we didn't expect to be so soon writing one about her.

Wendi's untimely passing in February 2022 left a great silent space in our group and in the Charlotte Mason community. Many remember Wendi because of the way that she promoted "the riches" of the curriculum, especially the inclusion of folk songs. She was often called on at retreats and conferences to speak on those topics, to read Hoosier poetry, or to teach a song. The several hundred parents and educators who attended the AO Camp Meeting in 2019 all went home humming "The Happy Wanderer," and it seems to be identified with her still.

However, before there was a Wendi famous for folk songs, there was Wendi who took on Charlotte Mason high school before it was commonly done. There was Wendi who, early on, became a prop and mainstay of the AO curriculum, putting countless hours into the creation of the upper years and challenging us to extend our multicultural vision while remaining true to Mason's principles. There was Moderator Wendi, who did not put up with much nonsense but was also patient and compassionate with moms who were struggling to make it work.

There was art-loving Wendi and literary Wendi, who had more books in her house than seemed physically possible and who snuck this description of Shakespeare into the biographical note: "His plays are memorable and speak to the universal human spirit. Never trust the literary opinions of anybody who says Shakespeare is not a big deal."

There was Wendi who challenged herself to learn enough ASL to interpret church services for a friend, who learned enough Korean to watch her favorite online dramas, and who later tackled Visaya as well (during two years of ministry in the Philippines).

There was Wendi who delighted in the nature-study potential of a Japanese island, the Pacific Northwest, and the woods and creeks of Indiana. There was frugal-homemaking Wendi, sharing recipes for large-family casseroles and homemade granola. (She found nothing pejorative in the term "crunchy.")

There was current-events Wendi, always aware of the best news bloggers and the stickiest human-rights issues. There was spiritual Wendi, deeply connected to her church and participating in ministry both to and from overseas countries. In 2012, she posted some "Tips for Frazzled and Busy Young Mothers" on her blog, *The Common Room*, including these suggestions: "Keep a book stand and a hymnal over the kitchen sink and sing hymns while washing dishes. Or print out a hymn and tape it to the window or wall behind the sink. If you're not into hymns, try folk songs."

There was Wendi who lived through more than her share of griefs and crises; who empathized (as she put it herself) with survivors of trauma; but who still reached out to others through postcards, crocheted toys, and all sorts of virtual (and real) hugs. She took on people. She took on projects. She took on Charlotte Mason with intelligence and enthusiasm.

And though it's impossible to capture all that was Wendi in such a brief sketch, we hope that she would not scoff too much at our attempt to say, "Never trust the opinion of anybody who says that Wendi Capehart was not a big deal."

(*First published in the* Common Place Quarterly, *volume 4, issue 4, October 2022. Used by permission.*)

# Tribute to Lynn

In Catherine Marshall's beautiful novel *Christy*, the young, idealistic teacher finds a scrap of paper on which her friend Fairlight Spencer had written these words:

> I love you for what you are making of me. I love you for what I am when I am with you. (p. 349)

Fairlight expresses how we felt about Lynn Bruce. And just as with Wendi, it's still a shock to write about Lynn in the past tense. We know she is with the Lord, but we are not. And that is the new space in which we now must walk.

Lynn grew up under the big Texas sky and under the preaching of her beloved Daddy. As a result, she knew the world God created and she knew the Word God gave us. Her knowledge about life was vast. It spanned an extravagant breadth that included knowing which books to read, which recipes to try, and what words to say, no matter the situation. She knew which hymns to sing, which Bible verses to quote, and which colors worked best (whether for lipstick, walls, websites, or flowers for our platform at AmblesideOnline Camp Meeting). And she was generous with that knowledge. She wanted us to know what she knew, to learn what she had learned, to see things as God had helped her to see them. She wanted each of us to do well, she wanted AmblesideOnline to be available for as many children as possible, and she wanted us to know that Jesus would go before us down every hard road.

Lynn's influence on AmblesideOnline is measured in beauty, encouragement, and friendship. She was a wordsmith who took great care that every phrase represented the ideas she had carefully studied. Whether it was in an article posted on our website, an account of her homeschool day written back when we were all on Charlotte Mason email lists, or a private letter shared only with us on the Advisory, Lynn always said things in a way that made us laugh, think, dream, and always remember. She was a storyteller, and she kept us in rapt attention through her emails, her speaking, and her writing.

Lynn prayed for us, loved us, delighted in us, and cheered us on. She daily marveled at God's astonishing grace. By her words and her example, she led us to see that grace as she did. Lynn took seriously the gift of life, and we were blessed to have a front-row seat to hers for the past two and a half decades. In her emails to us, she told us about every adventure, every joy, every valley. She told us to pray big, to grieve with hope, and to enjoy every sandwich. Lynn was dynamic, fun, and a fiercely loyal friend. It's easy to run out of words to describe her joyful presence and all that Lynn Bruce meant to us.

Lynn was larger than life. She loved so many people and was beloved back. But we were blessed beyond measure to be what she called her tribe, the impossible village of her heart. She was ever on our side, as she used to say, just as God was on hers. She knew how to rejoice when we rejoiced and to grieve when we grieved, even when her own pain was so constant and so intense.

Lynn pointed us to the Savior and to the sure promise of eternity. And one glad day, there will be a glorious reunion on God's celestial shore, in a land where joy shall never end. One glad day, we will see her again. One glad day, we will see Lynn and Wendi, and we will see Jesus.

Until then, dear friend.

## Donna-Jean: Enough

Picture this:

The table is full. There's a computer, there are notebooks and art prints—and stacks and stacks and stacks of books.

It's a typical summer scene, one that has been here in my kitchen for years. Dinner, if I can manage it during these weeks of planning, is spread on a picnic table out back or on trays on the porch. When I'm really in the thick of it, I have been known to mutter from behind a wall of history, biography, and free reads, "Fend for yourselves." There is organizing, combining, synchronizing, and tweaking the calendar. (Do I use the half week of Thanksgiving as a catch-up week? Do I spread that week over two weeks? How long do I stop for Christmas? Do I try for summer lessons or just admit it won't happen?)

And when I'm finally done with getting ready for the school year, I find that the beauty that is a Charlotte Mason / AmblesideOnline education looks abundant and very, very full.

Then a funny thing happens.

When the books find their way to the designated shelves, when the notebooks and supplies land in desks or in bins, when the calendar is in the laptop or phone or absorbed into a daybook, when the homeschool lessons actually begin—

Suddenly, everything changes. What was seen as so much, even a little daunting, morphs into inadequate. There is a temptation, even with a rich feast of a curriculum like AmblesideOnline, to use it as a base from which to do more.

Just read a poem a day? Yes, that's nice—but how about several poems read each day for comparison? What about researching the poem, looking for its literary devices, and defining vocabulary words? Surely several highlighters are needed, at least, maybe in a few different colors?

Literature? Great books are good, yes, but what about study guides or supplemental readings or, again, those lists of vocabulary words?

History? Is this the actual best prescribed rotation for the story of mankind? Shouldn't some of the tales from long ago and the uglier viewpoints of the past be left out? And why on earth start with the history of a country other than our own?

Nature study? Okay, but my little yard isn't all that exciting, and a walk in this neighborhood doesn't yield much to see—so isn't it best to add videos of nature, of important and real nature, and focus on stuff happening in rainforests and places far away?

Narration? Just "tell it back." Really? That's it? Isn't there more? Shouldn't it all be written down, corrected, recopied, and used for a study of the principles of composition?

Hymns and folk songs—just sing them? Don't we need musical analysis, the history of each work, and lots of hymn recitation?

And just like that, a path of freedom and beauty turns into drudgery and becomes instead a path towards burnout and exhaustion.

This feeling that more is needed is just that—a feeling. It bears no resemblance to the truth. I know this now because, well, I've been at this for a while. I've homeschooled this C.M./AO way since 1990, and the children whose curriculum plans were on my kitchen table this past summer include two of my three grandchildren—the ten- and seven-year-old daughters of the little girl I began to homeschool all those many years ago.

I've learned a lot of things through homeschooling my four children (three of them graduated, one still in high school) and now through helping to homeschool my grandchildren. And the main thing I've learned is this:

It is enough.

It is enough to park in the poetic mind of one man or woman for a season and hear their words read aloud, singly, daily, for the inspiration or challenge they bring. Before long, a student recognizes the poet's style, and a phrase or stanza or even the entire poem stays with that student—often for a lifetime.

It is enough to walk around the same yard, the same street, the same park or field, on a simple walk—and find that your child gets familiar with a single tree, with the sound of a returning bird, with the flow of a stream or brook, with the change of the seasons, with decay and renewal, and with wonder over God's creation. And the intense observation that comes from sketching a leaf, a feather, a nut, a web, or an animal track is the foundation and the essence of real science.

It is enough to read a book—not someone else's take on it. Imagine if you were given the choice of whether to stand in the front of the crowd and hear Abraham Lincoln give his second inaugural address or to read a political commentator's evaluation of it in a newspaper? It's the same with literature. There is simply no substitute for interaction with an author, for getting to know and witness firsthand the strength of the words and the force of the worldview.

It is enough to narrate—to use this powerful tool, even through the first steps of objections, last-word parroting, and missing facts. Very soon a pattern emerges out of the new habit, due to a strengthening of mind muscle, of attention, and of building associations. Blank stares are replaced with "This reminds me!" discoveries and connections with other books, history, life. And the analyzing, categorizing, connecting—and yes, the composing—is done by the child, not the study guide.

And it is enough to sing, just sing a hymn, and to learn to sing it even—maybe especially—without accompaniment. There may be no instruments available for your child when he walks in a hard place or wakes from a nightmare or waits for difficult news and finds comfort and guidance in singing quietly (or bravely), "When peace like a river attendeth my way, when sorrows like sea billows roll; whatever my lot, Thou hast taught me to say, 'It is well, it is well with my soul.'"

Some supports are used at times in an AO education, of course, such as a study guide for Plutarch, an introduction to a new book, or a more specific essay-style question for a narration. But the general Charlotte Mason principle that "the mind feeds on ideas, and therefore children should have a generous curriculum" (*A Philosophy of Education*, p. xxix) does not require for its implementation a paid advisor, an insider's interpretation of the six volumes, or a heretofore-unrevealed new approach to one subject or another. This method is well-tested, and many of us have lived the harvest of its beauty and simplicity.

So to the young mom whose table or laptop or library card or Amazon account has been full and who is daring to go forward but feeling a little bereft and uncertain without charts, unit studies, and workbooks—

Be reassured. It is enough.

To the harried homeschool teacher who's been at this for a while but whose life has gotten very tense and now high school looms large, with worry about tests and college and jobs and the future—

We've been there. It is enough.

And to the new homeschool mom whose children know facts but don't care and who is seeking for them to know Robert Louis Stevenson and Johann Sebastian Bach and William Shakespeare and, above all, the Bible, at least as well as or better than they know the current athletes, musicians, and celebrities—

Join us, and countless others. We've discovered—it is enough.

In fact, we've learned it's not just enough.

It is more than enough.

(*2017 post from* Archipelago)

# Epilogue

I've been thinking: What makes AO different from anything else in the educational world? The thing we must always remember, regardless of what is going on all around us, is that AO exists because Jesus gave this tiny band of women an inexplicable passion for handing Charlotte Mason's treasures over to poor people, to children on the mission field, to people in little trailer parks in Missouri who had old, lousy computers but wanted for their children an education that echoed heaven and all the good, timeless ideas that came from there. For the children's sake, yes, but for Jesus' sake over and above all...I feel the Spirit will be with us in this as long as we reckon with that anointing as being the sole source of the power that holds AO together and keeps it moving in the world. This thing is not us, and it is not ours. We are just the cracked vessels. (*Lynn Bruce, email, 2015*)

# Bibliography

Adams, Sir John. *The Herbartian Psychology Applied to Education.* London: D. C. Heath & Co., 1897.

Adler, Mortimer J., and Charles Van Doren. *How to Read a Book*. Rev. ed. New York: Simon & Schuster, 1996.

AO Advisory. Archipelago (blog). http://archipelago7.blogspot.com/.

AO Advisory. "Tribute to Wendi Capehart." *Common Place Quarterly* 4, no. 4 (October 2022): 65–66.

Augustine. *On Christian Doctrine.* Christian Classics Ethereal Library, 2005. https://www.ccel.org/ccel/augustine/doctrine.html.

Bestvater, Laurie. *The Living Page: Keeping Notebooks with Charlotte Mason.* Underpinnings Press, 2013.

Boswell, James. *The Project Gutenberg eBook of Life of Johnson*, Vol. 3. Edited by George Birkbeck Hill, https://www.gutenberg.org/cache/epub/9180/pg9180.html.

Browning, Oscar. *An Introduction to the History of Educational Theories.* 1902. Reprint, Routledge, 2015.

Chisholm, Thomas O. "Great is Thy Faithfulness," https://hymnary.org/text/great_is_thy_faithfulness_o_god_my_fathe.

Eliot, T. S. *Collected Poems 1909–1962.* London: Faber & Faber, 1974.

Elyot, Thomas. *The Boke Named the Governour.* 1531. Edited by Henry H. S. Croft. London: Kegan Paul, Trench, 1883.

Glass, Karen. *Consider This: Charlotte Mason and the Classical Tradition.* N.p., 2014.

Goudge, Elizabeth. *Pilgrim's Inn.* Peabody, MA: Hendrickson Publishers Marketing, LLC, 2013. (Published in London as *The Herb of Grace*, 1948.)

Hamblyn, Richard. *The Invention of Clouds: How an Amateur Meteorologist Forged the Language of the Skies.* London: Picador, 2011.

Herbert, George. *The English Poems of George Herbert.* Edited by Helen Wilcox. Cambridge, England: Cambridge University Press, 2011.

Household, H. W. *Notes for the Conference of July 18th, 1925 on P.N.E.U. Methods.* Gloucester, England: Crypt House Press, 1925.

K— (unknown). "How Firm a Foundation," https://hymnary.org/text/how_firm_a_foundation_ye_saints_of.

Katz, Steven, and Lisa A. Dack. *Intentional Interruption: Breaking Down Learning Barriers to Transform Professional Practice.* Thousand Oaks, CA: Corwin, 2013.

Kingsley, Charles. *Madam How and Lady Why, or, First Lessons in Earth Lore for Children.* New York: The Macmillan Company, 1901.

Laurio, Leslie. *Charlotte Mason Summaries.* N.p., 2005.

Laurio, Leslie. *Home Education in Modern English: Volume 1 of Charlotte Mason's Series.* N.p., 2005.

Laurio, Leslie. *Ourselves in Modern English: Volume 4 of Charlotte Mason's Series.* N.p., 2006.

Laurio, Leslie. *Parents and Children in Modern English: Volume 2 of Charlotte Mason's Series*. N.p., 2007.

Laurio, Leslie. *School Education in Modern English: Volume 3 of Charlotte Mason's Series*. N.p., 2006.

Laurio, Leslie. *Some Studies in the Formation of Character in Modern English: Volume 5 of Charlotte Mason's Series*. N.p., 2008.

Laurio, Leslie. *Towards a Philosophy of Education in Modern English: Volume 6 of Charlotte Mason's Series*. N.p., 2005.

Lewis, C. S. Introduction to *On the Incarnation,* by Saint Athanasius. Translated by John Behr. Yonkers, NY: St Vladimir's Seminary Press, 2011.

Lewis, C. S. "Meditation in a Toolshed." In *God in the Dock*, 212–215. Grand Rapids, MI: Eerdmans, 1998.

Macaulay, Susan S. *For the Children's Sake*. Wheaton, IL: Crossway Books, 1984.

MacDonald, George. *The Princess and Curdie*. London: Strahan & Co., 1883.

Marshall, Catherine. *Christy*. New York: Avon Books, 1967.

Mason, Charlotte M. *Formation of Character*. Vol. 5 of *The Original Home Schooling Series*. Wheaton, IL: Tyndale House, 1989. Originally published 1906 as *Some Studies in the Formation of Character* by Kegan Paul, Trench, Trubner and Co., Ltd. (London). Page references are to the 1989 edition.

Mason, Charlotte M. *Home Education*. Vol. 1 of *The Original Home Schooling Series*. Wheaton, IL: Tyndale House, 1989. Originally published 1935 by Kegan Paul, Trench, Trubner and Co., Ltd. (London). Page references are to the 1989 edition.

Mason, Charlotte M. *Ourselves*. Vol. 4 of *The Original Home Schooling Series*. Wheaton, IL: Tyndale House, 1989. Originally published 1905 by Kegan Paul, Trench, Trubner and Co., Ltd. (London). Page references are to the 1989 edition.

Mason, Charlotte M. *Parents and Children.* Vol. 2 of *The Original Home Schooling Series.* Wheaton, IL: Tyndale House, 1989. Originally published 1904 by Kegan Paul, Trench, Trubner and Co., Ltd. (London). Page references are to the 1989 edition.

Mason, Charlotte M. *A Philosophy of Education.* Vol. 6 of *The Original Home Schooling Series.* Wheaton, IL: Tyndale House, 1989. Originally published 1925 as *An Essay Towards a Philosophy of Education* by Kegan Paul, Trench, Trubner and Co., Ltd. (London). Page references are to the 1989 edition.

Mason, Charlotte M. *School Education.* 1904. Reprint, Wheaton, IL: Tyndale House, 1989. Originally published 1907 by Kegan Paul, Trench, Trubner and Co., Ltd. (London). Page references are to the 1989 edition.

McKeown, Greg. *Essentialism: The Disciplined Pursuit of Less.* New York: Crown Business, 2014.

Milne, A. A. *The House at Pooh Corner.* New York: Dutton Children's Books, 1988.

Moffatt, James. *Life of Thomas Chalmers.* Princeton, NJ: College of New Jersey, 1851.

Parents' National Educational Union. *In Memoriam.* London: PNEU, 1923.

Perelman, Deb. "Double Chocolate Banana Bread." Smitten Kitchen. March 17, 2014. https://smittenkitchen.com/2014/03/double-chocolate-banana-bread/.

Pieper, Josef. *Leisure: the Basis of Culture.* Translated by Gerald Malsbary. South Bend, IN: St. Augustine's Press, Inc., 1998.

Rooper, Thomas Godolphin. *Educational Studies and Addresses*. London: Blackie & Son, 1902.

Sammis, John H. "Trust and Obey," https://hymnary.org/media/fetch/138917.

Spafford, Horatio Gates. "When Peace, Like a River," https://hymnary.org/text/when_peace_like_a_river_attendeth_my_way.

Tolkien, J. R. R. *The Fellowship of the Ring*. Vol. 1, The Lord of the Rings. London: HarperCollins, 1991.

Tolkien, J. R. R. *The Two Towers*. Vol. 2, The Lord of the Rings. London: HarperCollins, 1991.

Warner, Anna Bartlett. "Jesus Loves Me." *Bradbury's Golden Shower of S. S. Melodies: A New Collection of Hymns and Tunes for the Sabbath School*. Edited by Wm. B. Bradbury. New York: Ivison, Phinney & Co., 1862.

Vanauken, Sheldon. *A Severe Mercy*. London, Sydney, Auckland, Toronto: Hodder & Stoughton, 1977.

White, Anne E. *Minds More Awake: The Vision of Charlotte Mason* (Revised Edition). N.p., 2021.

Whitehead, Alfred North. *The Aims of Education*. New York: Mentor Books, 1961.

Wordsworth, William. *The Prelude or Growth of a Poet's Mind*. London: J.M. Dent.

Yeats, William Butler. "The Lake Isle of Innisfree." Untermeyer, Louis. *Modern British Poetry*. New York, Harcourt, Brace and Howe, 1920; Bartleby.com, 1999. www.bartleby.com/103/.

Made in the USA
Middletown, DE
01 September 2024